NEGRO WORKADAY SONGS

BY

HOWARD W. ODUM, Ph.D.

*Kenan Professor of Sociology and Director of
the School of Public Welfare, University of
North Carolina*

AND

GUY B. JOHNSON, A.M.

*Institute for Research in Social Science,
University of North Carolina*

NEGRO UNIVERSITIES PRESS
NEW YORK

The Library of Congress cataloged this book as follows:

Odum, Howard Washington, 1884–1954.
 Negro workaday songs, by Howard W. Odum and Guy
B. Johnson. New York, Negro Universities Press ₍1969₎

 xii, 278 p. illus., music. 23 cm.

 Half title: The University of North Carolina. Social study series.
 Reprint of the 1926 ed.
 Bibliography: p. ₍265₎–270.

 1. Negro songs. 2. Negro songs—History and criticism. ɪ. Johnson, Guy Benton, 1901– joint author. ɪɪ. Title. (Series: North
Carolina. University. Social study series)

ML3556.O32 1969   784.7′56   78–89050
SBN 8371–1938–3   MARC

Library of Congress   69 ₍2₎   MN

Originally published in 1926 by the University of North
Carolina Press

Reprinted by Greenwood Press, Inc.

First reprinted in 1969 by Negro Universities Press
Second reprinting 1977

Library of Congress catalog card number 78-89050
ISBN 0-8371-1938-3

Printed in the United States of America

THE UNIVERSITY OF NORTH CAROLINA

SOCIAL STUDY SERIES

NEGRO WORKADAY SONGS

A vast throng of Negro workaday singers, mirrors of a race

Workingmen in the Southern United States from highway, construction camp, from railroad and farm, from city and countryside, a million strong

A half million migrants from the South, Eastward, Northward, Westward, and some South again

Negro offenders in thousand fold in local jails, county chain gangs, state and federal prisons

A horde of Southern casual laborers and wanderers down that lonesome road

A brown black army of "bad men"— creepers and ramblers and jamboree breakers, "travelin' men" de luxe

Itinerant full-handed musicianers, music physicianers and songsters, singly, in pairs, quartets, always moving on

A host of women workers from field and home and factory at once singers and subjects of the lonesome blues

A swelling crescendo, a race vibrato inimitable, descriptive index of group character, folk urge and race power

PREFACE

Negro Workaday Songs is the third volume of a series of folk background studies of which *The Negro and His Songs* was the first and *Folk-Beliefs of the Southern Negro* was the second. The series will include a number of other volumes on the Negro and likewise a number presenting folk aspects of other groups. The reception which the first volumes have received gives evidence that the plan of the series to present scientific, descriptive, and objective studies in as interesting and readable form as possible may be successful in a substantial way. Since the data for background studies are, for the time being, practically unlimited, it is hoped that other volumes, appearing as they become available and timely, may glimpse the whole range—from the Negro "bad man" to the æsthetic in the folk urge.

In this volume, as in previous ones, the emphasis is primarily social, although this indicates no lack of appreciation of the inherent literary and artistic values of the specimens presented. Indeed, so far as possible, all examples of folk expression in this volume are left to tell their own story. The type melodies and musical notations are presented separately with the same descriptive purpose as the other chapters, and they are not offered as a substitute for effective harmonies and musical interpretation. For the purposes of this volume, however, the separate chapters on the melodies and phono-photographic records with musical notations are very important. It is also important that they be studied separately, but in the light of the preceding chapters, rather than inserted in the text to detract from both the social and artistic interpretation of the songs enumerated.

The Seashore-Metfessel phono-photographic records and musical notations mark an important contribution to the whole field of interpretation of Negro music. There may be an outstanding contribution both to the musical world and to the whole interpretation of Negro backgrounds in the possible thesis that the Negro, in addition to his distinctive contribution to harmony, excels also in the vibrato quality of the individual voice. These studies were made at Chapel Hill and at Hampton by Dr. Carl E. Seashore and Dr. Milton Metfessel of the University of Iowa, under the auspices of the Institute for Research in Social Science at the University of North Carolina through a special grant of the Laura Spelman Rockefeller Memorial. Full acknowledgment to them is here made.

It should be kept constantly in mind that this volume, like *The Negro and His Songs*, is in no sense an anthology or general collection, but represents the group of songs *current in certain areas in North Carolina, South Carolina, Tennessee and Georgia,* during the years 1924-25. Of course all of this collection cannot be included in this volume; and no doubt many of the most important or most attractive specimens extant have escaped us at this time. It is also important to note that in this volume, as in the previous one, all speciments listed, except lines or references otherwise designated, *were taken directly from Negro singers* and do not represent reports from memory of white individuals. So far as we know none of the songs in this collection has been published, although there are countless variations, adaptations and corruptions of the modern blues and jazz songs represented in the group. The songs, however, *were all*

sung or repeated by actual Negro workers or singers,
and much of their value lies in the exact transcription
of natural lines, words, and mixtures. The collection
is still growing by leaps and bounds. In this volume
every type is represented except the "dirty dozen"
popular models and the more formal and sophisticated
creations.

Since this volume presents a series of pictures of the
Negro as portrayed through his workaday songs it is
important that all chapters be read before any final
judgment is made. Even then the picture will not be
complete. It has not been possible, of course, to make
any complete or accurate classification of the songs.
They overlap and repeat. They borrow sentiment and
expression and repay freely. Free labor song becomes
prison song, and chain gang melody turns to pick-and-
shovel accompaniment. The chapter divisions, therefore, are made with the idea of approximating a usable
classification and providing such mechanical divisions
as will facilitate the best possible presentation.

The reader who approaches this volume from the
point of view of the technical student of folk song will
likely be disappointed at what he considers the lack
of discrimination displayed by the authors in admitting
so many songs which cannot be classed as strictly folk
songs. We have frankly taken the position that these
semi-folk songs, crude and fragmentary, and often
having only local or individual significance, afford
even more accurate pictures of Negro workaday life
and art than the conventional folk songs. While we
have spared no effort to make the collection valuable
for folk song students, we have approached the work
primarily as sociologists.

For assistance in recording the type melodies in Chapter XIV we are specially indebted to Mr. Lee M. Brooks, and for many of the songs of women to Mrs. Henry Odum. We wish to thank Mr. Gerald W. Johnson for his goodness in going over much of the manuscript and making valuable suggestions. To Dr. L. R. Wilson, Director of the University of North Carolina Press, we are much indebted for coöperation and suggestions.

CHAPEL HILL
January, 1926

H. W. O.
G. B. J.

CONTENTS

NEGRO WORKADAY SONGS

CHAPTER I

BACKGROUND RESOURCES IN NEGRO SONG AND WORK

To discover and present authentic pictures of the Negro's folk background as found in his workaday songs is a large and promising task of which there are many phases. Here are spontaneous products of the Negro's workaday experiences and conflicts. Here are reflections of his individual strivings and his group ways. Here are specimens of folk art and creative effort close to the soil. Here are new examples of the Negro's contributions to the American scene. Here is important material for the newer scientific interest which is taking the place of the old sentimental viewpoint. And here is a mine of descriptive and objective data to substitute for the emotional and subjective attitudes of the older days.

It is a day of great promise in the United States when both races, North and South, enter upon a new era of the rediscovery of the Negro and face the future with an enthusiasm for facts, concerning both the newer creative urge and the earlier background sources. Concerning the former, Dr. Alain Locke recently has said:[1] "Whoever wishes to see the Negro in his essential traits, in the full perspective of his achievement and possibilities, must seek the enlightenment of that self-portraiture which the present development of the Negro culture offers." One of the best examples of that self-portraiture is that of the old spirituals, long neglected, but now happily the subject of a new race dedication and appreciation. Now comes another

---

[1] *The New Negro*, edited by Alain Locke.

master index of race temperament and portrayal, as found in some of the Negro's newer creations. No less important, from the viewpoint of sheer originality and poetic effort as well as of indices of traits and possibilities, are the seemingly unlimited mines of workaday songs, weary blues, and black man ballads. In a previous volume [1] we presented a sort of composite picture from two hundred songs gathered two decades ago and interpreted with something of prophetic evaluation. In this volume of Negro Workaday Songs is presented a deeper mine of source material, rich in self-portraiture and representative of the workaday Negro.

In his *Peter the Czar*, violent story of "lashed sentences," perfectly suited to the depiction of primitive character, Klabund pictures vividly a certain Great Enemy about whose "shivering shoulders lay a rainbow like a silken shawl." Digging to the syncopated rhythm of song and fast-whirling pick, a Negro workman sings of another rainbow, equally vivid and shoulder-draped, more concrete, personal, and real:

> Ev'ywhere I look this,
> Ev'ywhere I look this mo'nin',
> Looks like rain.
>
> I got rainbow
> Tied 'round my shoulder,
> Ain't gonna rain,
> Lawd, ain't gonna rain. [2]

In addition to the poetic imagery in this seemingly unconscious motor-minded product, one may glimpse evidences of simple everyday experience, wishful thought, childlike faith, workaday stolidity, physical

---

[1] *The Negro and His Songs*, by Howard W. Odum and Guy B. Johnson.
[2] Musical notation will be found in Chapter XIV.

satisfaction, and subtle humor. But he can find still more humor and experience, with a good bit of metaphor thrown in for good measure, in the "feet rollin'" stanza of another wanderer's song of the road:

> I done walk till,
> Lawd, I done walk till
> Feet's gone to rollin',
> Jes' lak a wheel,
> Lawd, jes' lak a wheel.

Resourcefulness, humor, defense mechanism, imagination, all might be found in the spectacle of a group of Negroes singing over and over again on a hot July day the refreshing lines,

> Oh, next winter gonna be so cold,
> Oh, next winter gonna be so cold,
> Oh, next winter gonna be so cold,
> Fire can't warm you, be so cold.

With the thermometer around a hundred, and the work of digging at hand, this song of "parts," with some of the singers using the words, "be so cold, be so cold" as an echo, undoubtedly had peculiar merit.

Perhaps there have been few, if any, lines of poetry more popular than Wordsworth's "The light that never was on sea or land." The Negro worker sings of a more earthly yet equally miraculous light to guide his pathway, when he complains,

> Now ev'y time I,
> Time I start 'round mountain,
> My light goes out,
> Lawd, Lawd, my light goes out.
>
> I'm gonna buy me,
> Buy me magnified lantern,

> It won't go out,
> Lawd, Lawd, it won't go out.

How much of symbolism is to be found in the Negro's workaday songs? How much subjective imagery, how much unconscious allegory? There are abundant examples of the free use of symbolism in his love songs and popular jazz appeals. But what does he mean when he sings,

> Ever see wild cat
> Hug a lion, Lawd, Lawd?
>
> My ol' bear cat
> Turn to lion, Lawd, Lawd.
>
> Ever see lion
> Run lak hell, Lawd, Lawd?

Or contrast this simple individual song, with its humor and easy-going rhythm, with the power and appeal of group singing. Here is a goodly party of two-score white folk, seated at twilight under the trees in a grove, joyous guests at a turkey dinner near the old colonial home. There is merriment. Song and jest, toast and cheer abound. The waiters have gone. Then from the kitchen door comes the song of Negroes, beginning low, rising in volume, telling of the sinking of the Titanic. What is it in that final harmony of "God moved upon the waters," sung by a Negro group, which silenced the merrymakers into willing recognition that here may be perfect art and perfect effect? Does this Negro minstrel type, rendered thus in native setting, become for the moment the perfect expression of folk spirit and folk art?

Hundreds of verses dedicated to the business of moving about give evidence that the trail of the black knight of the road is strewn with spontaneous song, often turned into polished phrase. A favorite stanza has long been descriptive of being "on road here few days longer, then I'll be going home." Sung again and again, the song takes on a new form but loses nothing of its emphatic meaning:

> I'm gonna row here,
> I'm gonna row here
> Few days longer,
> Then I'll be gone,
> Lawd, I'll be gone.

For, says the worker, "If I feel tomorrow like I feel today, I'm gonna pack my suitcase and walk away," and "reason I'm workin' here so long, hot flambotia and coffee strong."

Following the trail of the workaday Negro, therefore, one may get rare glimpses of common backgrounds of Negro life and experience in Southern communities. Here were the first real plantings of the modern blues, here songs of the lonesome road, here bad man ballads, here distinctive contributions in songs of jail and chain gang, here songs of white man and captain, here Negro Dr. Jekyls and Mr. Hydes. Here are found new expressions of the old spirituals and remnants still surviving. Here man's song of woman is most varied and original, and woman's song of man is best echoed from days and nights of other times. Here àre reflected the epics of John Henry, Lazarus, Dupree, and the others. Here are folk fragments, cries and "hollers," songs to help with work, physical satisfaction and solace, the "Lawdy-Lawdy" vibrato of evening melancholy and morning yodel. Here may be found the subliminal jazz, rare rhythm and movement, coöperative harmony as characteristic as ever the old spirituals revealed. Nevertheless, too much emphasis cannot be placed upon the danger of over-interpretation, for while the workaday songs provide a seemingly exhaustive supply of mirror plate for the reflection of folk temperament and struggle, too much analysis must not obscure their vividness or the beauty and value of their intrinsic qualities.

It is important to note the extent to which the notable popular blues of today, more formal embodiment of the Negro's workaday sorrow songs, have come from these workaday products. Here are true descendants of the old worshipers who sang so well of the Rock in a weary land. And echoing from Southern distances, from Memphis and Natchez, from New Orleans and Macon, from Charleston and Atlanta, and from wayside roads and camps, from jail and chain gang, come unmeasured volume of harmony, unnumbered outbursts of song, perfect technique of plaintive appeal. Many of the most plaintive lines of blues yet recorded were gathered decades ago from camp and road in Mississippi before the technique of the modern blues had ever been evolved. Eloquent successors to the old spirituals with their sorrow-feeling, these songs of the lonesome road have gathered power and numbers and artistic interpretation until they defy description and record. Today the laborer, the migrant, the black man offender constitute types as distinctive and inimitable as the old jubilee singers and those whom they represented. Wherever Negroes work, or loaf, or await judgment, there may be heard the weary and lonesome blues so strange and varied as to reveal a sort of superhuman evidence of the folk soul. No amount of ordinary study into race backgrounds, or historical annals of African folk, or elaborate anthropological excursions can give so simply and completely the story of this Negro quest for expression, freedom, and solace as these low-keyed melancholy songs.

And what names and lines, words and melodies, records and improvisations of the new race blues! Plaintive blues, jolly blues, reckless blues, dirty dozen blues, mama blues, papa blues,—more than six hundred listed by one publisher and producer. Here they are— the workaday sorrow songs, the errant love songs, the jazz lyrics of a people and of an age—as clearly distinctive as the old spirituals. And how like the road songs and the gang lines, straight up from the soil again, straight from the folk as surely as ever came the old spirituals.

Samples of the growing list of blues, some less elegant, some more aggressive, will be found in Chapter II. And of course we must not forget the bad man blues: *Dangerous Blues, Evil Blues, Don't Mess With Me Blues, Mean Blues, Wicked Blues*, and most of all the *Chain Gang Blues, Jail Blues*, and the *Cell-bound Blues*.

> All boun' in prison,
> All boun' in jail,
> Col' iron bars all 'roun' me,
> No one to pay my bail.

And the singer presents, as one of his standard versions of many songs, a regular weekly calendar:

> Monday I was 'rested,
> Tuesday I was fined,
> Wednesday I laid in jail,
> Thursday I was tried,
> Friday wid chain gang band,
> Saturday pick an' shovel,
> Sunday I took my rest,
> Monday wanta do my best.

Perhaps the most common concept found in the chain gang and road songs and appearing here and there in all manner of song is the concept of a letter from home, the inability to go home without "ready money," the attempt to borrow from the captain, or to get a parole.

Every, every mail day,
I gits letter from my mother,
Cryin', "Son, come home,
Lawdy, son, come home."

I didn't have no,
No ready-made money,
I couldn't go home,
Lawd, couldn't go home.

A constant source of song is the conflict between actual conditions and desirable ends, between life as it is and ideals of wishful dreaming. "I want to go home," says the workman, but "I don't want no trouble wid de walker." The resulting product is absence from home, absence of trouble with the captain or walker, and abundance of song.

I don't want no trouble,
I don't want no trouble,
I don't want no trouble wid de walker.
Lawd, Lawd, I wanta go home.

Me an' my buddy jes' come,
Me an' my buddy jes' come,
Me an' my buddy jes' come here.
Lawd, Lawd, wanta go home.

Again and again the Negro wanderer portrays home, parents, brothers and sisters, friends, as the most highly esteemed of life's values—striking paradox to the realism of his practice. Idealism in song and dreams, in workaday songs as well as spirituals, alongside sordidness in living conditions and physical surroundings, appear logical and direct developments from the type of habitation which the Negro common man has ever known.

The Negro "bad man" who sings sorrowfully of his mother's admonitions and his own mistakes, glories also in the motor-imaged refrain:

> In come a nigger named Billy Go-helf,
> Coon wus so mean wus skeered uf hisself;
> Loaded wid razors an' guns, so they say,
> 'Cause he killed a coon most every day.

A later chapter is devoted to this notable character, the "bad man," whose varied pictures represent a separate Negro contribution. Here are new and worthy Negro exhibits to add to the American galaxy of folk portraits: Railroad Bill alongside Jesse James, the Negro "bad man" beside the Western frontiersman, and John Henry by Paul Bunyan. For from the millions of Negroes of yesterday and as many more today, with their oft-changing and widely varying economic and social conditions, has come a rare and varied heritage of folk tradition, folk character, and folk personality. Much of this might remain forever unknown and unsung were it not for the treasure-house of Negro song, the product of a happy facility for linking up the realities of actual life with wishful thinking and imaginative story.

Of the grand old "saints," white haired "Uncles" and "Aunties," we have viewed from near and far scores of inimitable examples. Of the thousands of musicianers, songsters and workers, and those who sing "down that lonesome road," recent epochs have mirrored many. But what of the real and mythical jamboree breakers and bad men, or of Po' Lazarus and

Stagolee, or of John Henry, "forehanded steel-drivin' man" and ideal of the Negro worker?

Here are rare folk figures silhouetted against a sort of shifting race background with its millions of working folk and wanderers moving suddenly and swiftly across the scene. A brown-black army of ramblers, creepers, high flyers, standin' men, all-night workers, polish men, "stick and ready" from the four corners of the States—Lazarus, Billy Bob Russel, Shootin' Bill, Brady, Dupree, and the others. And then John Henry, stately and strong in contrast, noble exponent of sturdy courage and righteous struggle, faithful to death.

> John Henry went to the mountain,
> Beat that steam-drill down;
> Rock was high, po' John was small,
> He laid down his hammer an' he died,
> Laid down his hammer an' he died.

A chapter on "Man's Song of Woman" will make but a small beginning of a large task. Its sequel must be deferred until the lover's specialisms can be published with a liberal usage of the psychiatrists' terminology. A chapter on "Woman's Song of Man" ought also to have a companion sequel in the book of Negro symbolism. A chapter on "Workaday Religious Songs" can present only a small portion of those now being sung, but will be representative of the present heritage of the old spirituals. A chapter on the miscellaneous fragments, "hollers," lines, incoherent and expressive "Lawdy-Lawd-Lawds" gives one of the best pictures of the Negro workaday character and habits. Some of these types make a very good safety valve for the Negro singer; in a different way their plainness may restrain the enthusiast from setting too much "store" by all the Negro's songs. The characters of John Henry and

Left Wing represent two types, one the mythical and heroic, the other the real and commonplace, both typical of the Negro's idealism and his actual life. The examples of "movement and imagery" are as characteristic of the Negro workaday experience as were the harmonies and swaying of the old spirituals. They are indices to guide judgment and interpretation of the Negro temperament. In each of these chapters, it will be understood, only enough material is presented to illustrate the case, including, however, always the most representative specimens which the authors have been able to collect within their field and time limit. Much that is similar will necessarily await publication in volumes in which the chief objective will be preservation and completeness rather than interpretation.

Many pictures of the workaday Negro are presented in this volume through the medium of his songs. They are silhouetted, as it were, at first against a complex background of Negro life and experience. The pictures are vivid, concrete, distinct, often complete. But most of all, perhaps, they have been *moving* pictures. From the first glimpse of the Negro singer with his "feet's gone to rollin' jes' lak a wheel," to the last great scene of John Henry dying with the "hammer in his hand," there is marvelous movement alongside rare imagery. Sometimes rhythm and rhyme, but always movement, have dominated the Negro's chief characterizations. And this movement in the workaday songs is as much a distinctive feature as were the swaying bodies, the soothing rhythm, and swelling harmony of the old spirituals. Picture the Negro workingman in his song and story life and you picture him on the move.

It is scarcely possible to describe this element of movement in the Negro workaday songs. And yet the mere citation and classification of representative examples will suffice to point out the particular qualities of action which might justify the added element of epic style, if one remembers that the singer's concept of the heroic, while very real, is not exalted in the Greek sense. There are those who do not feel that the Negro's workaday songs are characterized by the qualities of poetry; yet do they not arouse the feelings and imagination in vivid and colorful language? The type of language used—that is the Negro's own. In the same way there can be no doubt of his songs emphasizing the quality of action; his heroes and principal figures, like his language, reflect his concepts and tell his stories. Whether epic or heroic,

> I'm the hot stuff man,
> From the devil's land,
> I'm a greasy streak o' lightning,
> Don't you see, don't you see?

has plenty of action and imagery in it. And it is characteristic of much of the Negro workaday style of talk, imagination, and thought.

Many of the pictures are vivid because of the action concept and the rhyming metaphors.

> In come a nigger named Slippery Jim,
> None of de gals would dance wid him,
> He rech in his pocket an' drew his thirty-two,
> Dem niggers didn't rŭn, good Gawd, dey flew.

There was also a woman, one Eliza Stone, from a bad, bad land, who threatened to break up the jamboree with her razor but who also "jumped in de flo', an' doubled up her fist, say 'You wanter test yo' nerve jes' jump against this.'" Note further a varying reel of moving characters and scenes.

Police got into auto
An' started to chase that coc‐
They run 'im from six in the mo'nin',
Till seven that afternoon.

The coon he run so bloomin' fas'
Till fire come from his heels,
He scorched the cotton an' burnt the corn,
An' cut a road through farmers' fiel's.

The continuous search after the workaday folk song will always provide one of the most important guides to the "discovery" of the Negro. The task of finding and recording accurately the folk expression is a difficult one under most circumstances. Under certain circumstances it is an easy task, and always an interesting one. If we keep a record of efforts, taken at random, as experimental endeavor, in a cross country visit through North Carolina, South Carolina, Tennessee and Georgia, about ten per cent, at best, of the requests for songs will be successful. There are other times, when setting and procedure are worked out well, when almost one hundred per cent success would be attained. In most instances the Negro is at his "best" when being urged to coöperate in the rendering of his folk songs. By his "best" is meant that he reveals a striking nature and strong personality, whether in affirming stoutly that he knows no songs now or that he has forgotten what he used to know. He protests vigorously that he does not sing well enough, that he cannot say the words of songs unless he can sing, that he cannot sing unless others are singing, that he has to be in the spirit of the song, or that he will get some songs together and bring them in, or that he will bring a quartet or a pal. Rarely ever does he "produce" if let alone with only a first approach. Nor can he be blamed. He is entirely within his own self-protecting domain, so that his attitude may be put down, not only as a characteristic one but also as a commendable one. He has his own fun, too, in the situation. In general there are several types from which little success may be expected. The more educated and sophisticated Negro not only does not as a rule coöperate, but looks with considerable condescension upon those who seek his help. There are many who believe that all songs desired are for immediate transcription to printed music or phonograph record. These are of little assistance. Others feel that some hidden motive is back of the request. Still others for various reasons do not coöperate. Nor will the Negro student or musician himself find ready coöperation among his common folk who feel constrained to withhold their folk art from the learned of their own race.

Perhaps the most striking observation that comes from the whole experience is the seemingly inexhaustible supply of songs among the workaday Negroes of the South. We have yet to find a "bottom" or a limit in the work songs among the crowds of working men in one community. Just as often as there is opportunity to hear a group of Negroes singing at work, just so often have we found new songs and new fragments. There is so far no exception to this rule. Likewise we have yet to find an individual, whose efforts have been freely set forth in the offering of song, whose supply of songs has been exhausted. Time and time again the approach has been made, with the response, "Naw, sir, cap'n, I don't know no songs much," with an ultimate result of song after song, seemingly with no limit. Partly the singer is honest; he does not at the time, think of many songs nor does he consider himself a good singer; but when he turns himself "loose" his capacity for memory and singing is astonishing.

The same general rule with reference to dialect is used in this volume as was the case in *The Negro and His Songs*. [1] There can be no consistency, except the consistency of recording the words as nearly as possible as rendered. Words may occur in two or three variations in a single stanza and sometimes in a single line. The attempt to make formal dialect out of natural speech renders the product artificial and less artistic. We have therefore followed the general practice of keeping the dialect as simple as possible. Dialect, after all, is a relative matter. It is the sort of speech which is not used in one's own section of the country. As a matter of fact, much of what has passed as Negro dialect is good white Southern usage, and there is nothing to justify the attempt to set aside certain pronunciations as peculiar to the Negro simply because a Negro is being quoted. Consequently we have refrained from the use of dialect in all cases where the Negro pronunciation and the usual white pronunciation are the same or practically the same. If the reader will grasp the basic points of difference between Negro and white speech and will then keep in mind the principle of economy, he will have no difficulty in following the peculiarities of dialect.

The principle of economy will be found to operate at high efficiency in Negro speech. It will nearly always explain the apparent inconsistencies in dialect. For example, the Negro often says *'bout* and *'roun'* for *about* and *around*. But he might vary these to *about, aroun', 'round,* and *around* in a single song, depending upon the preceding and succeeding sounds. He would say, "I'll go *bout* two o'clock," but he

---

[1] *The Negro and His Songs*, pp. 9-11, 293-94. There is a good discussion of dialect in James Weldon Johnson's *Book of American Negro Spirituals*, pp. 42-46.

also would say, "I went about two o'clock," because in the former case it is easier to say *'bout* than *about*, while in the latter the reverse is true.

Rhythm is also related to dialect. In ordinary speech most Negroes would say *broke* for *broken*, but if the rhythm in singing called for a two-syllable sound they would say *broken* rather than *broke*.

Very few of the popular songs which we heard twenty years ago are found now in the same localities. The places that knew them will know them no more. The same disappearing process is going on now, only more rapidly than formerly because of the multitude of blues, jazz songs, and others being distributed throughout the land in millions of phonographic records. One of the first tasks of this volume is, therefore, to take cognizance of these formal blues, both in their relation to the workaday native creations and as an important segment of the Negro's music and his contribution to the American scene. In the next chapter we shall proceed, therefore, to discuss the blues.

CHAPTER II

THE BLUES: WORKADAY SORROW SONGS

No story of the workaday song life of the Negro can proceed far without taking into account the kind of song known as the blues, for, next to the spirituals, the blues are probably the Negro's most distinctive contribution to American art. They have not been taken seriously, because they have never been thoroughly understood. Their history needs to be written. The present chapter is not a complete statement. It merely presents some of the salient points in the story of the blues and offers some suggestions as to their rôle in Negro life.

Behind the popular blues songs of today lie the more spontaneous and naïve songs of the uncultured Negro. Long before the blues were formally introduced to the public, the Negro was creating them by expressing his gloomy moods in song. To be sure, the present use of the term "blues" to designate a particular kind of popular song is of recent origin, but the use of the term in Negro song goes much further back, and the blue or melancholy type of Negro secular song is as old as the spirituals themselves. The following song might be taken at first glance for one of the 1926 popular "hits," but it dates back to the time of the Civil War. [1]

> I'm gwine to Alabamy,—Oh,
> For to see my mammy,—Ah.

---

[1] Allen, Ware, and Garrison, *Slave Songs of the United States*, p. 89; This note is appended: "A very good specimen . . . of the strange barbaric songs that one hears upon the Western steamboats."

She went from ole Virginny,—Oh,
And I'm her pickaniny,—Ah.

She lives on the Tombigbee,—Oh,
I wish I had her wid me,—Ah.

Now I'm a good big nigger,—Oh,
I reckon I won't git bigger,—Ah,

But I'd like to see my mammy,—Oh
Who lives in Alabamy,—Ah.

Very few of the Negro's ante-bellum secular songs
have been preserved, but there is every reason to suppose that he had numerous melancholy songs aside
from the spirituals.   At any rate, the earliest authentic secular collections abound in the kind of songs which
have come to be known as the blues.   The following
expressions are typical of the early blues.   They are
taken from songs collected in Georgia and Mississippi
between 1905 and 1908, and they were doubtless
common property among the Negroes of the lower
class long before that. [1]

Went to the sea, sea look so wide,
Thought about my babe, hung my head an' cried.
O my babe, won't you come home?

I got the blues, but too damn mean to cry,
Oh, I got the blues, but I'm too damn mean to cry.

Got nowhar to lay my weary head,
O my babe, got nowhar to lay my weary head.

I'm po' boy long way from home,
Oh, I'm po' boy long way from home.

Ever since I left dat country farm,
Ev'ybody been down on me.

---

[1] This collection was published by Howard W. Odum in the *Journal of American Folk-Lore*, vol. 24, pp. 255-94; 351-96.

Here are blues in the making. This is the stuff that the first published blues were made of, and some of it sounds strikingly like certain of the latest blues records issued by the phonograph companies. About 1910 the first published blues appeared, and since that time they have been exploited in every imaginable form by music publishers and phonograph companies. [1] The inter-relations between the formal blues and the native blues will be discussed later. At present it is necessary to take up certain questions concerning the nature of the blues.

What are the characteristics of the native blues, in so far as they can be spoken of as a type of song apart from other Negro songs? The original blues were so fragmentary and elusive—they were really little more than states of mind expressed in song—that it is difficult to characterize them definitely. The following points, then, are merely suggestive.

In the first place, blues are characterized by a tone of plaintiveness. Both words and music give the impression of loneliness and melancholy. In fact, it was this quality, combined with the Negro's peculiar use of the word "blues," which gave the songs their name. In the second place, the theme of most blues is that of the love relation between man and woman. There are many blues built around homesickness and hard luck in general, but the love theme is the principal one. Sometimes the dominant note is the complaint of the lover:

---

[1] W. C. Handy is credited with having published the first blues (*Memphis Blues*, 1910) and with having had much to do with their popularization. He is still writing songs. His works include *Memphis Blues, St. Louis Blues, Beale St. Blues, Joe Turner Blues, Yellow Dog Blues, Aunt Hagar's Blues,* and others.

> Goin' 'way to leave you, ain't comin' back no mo',
> You treated me so dirty, ain't comin' back no mo'. [1]

> Where was you las' Sattaday night,
> When I lay sick in bed?
> You down town wid some other ol' girl,
> Wusn't here to hol' my head. [2]

Sometimes it is a note of longing:

> I hate to hear my honey call my name,
> Call me so lonesome and so sad. [3]

> I believe my woman's on that train,
> O babe, I believe my woman's on that train. [4]

At other times the dominant note is one of disappointment:

> I thought I had a friend was true;
> Done found out friends won't do. [5]

> All I hope in this bright worl',
> If I love anybody, don't let it be a girl. [6]

A third characteristic of the blues is the expression of self pity. [7] Often this is the outstanding feature of the song. There seems to be a tendency for the despondent or blue singer to use the technique of the martyr to draw from others a reaction of sympathy. Psychologically speaking, the technique consists of rationalization, by which process the singer not only excuses his shortcomings, but attracts the attention and sympathy of others—in imagination, at least—

---

[1] *The Negro and His Songs*, p. 184.
[2] *Ibid.*, p. 185.
[3] *Ibid.*, p. 224.
[4] *Ibid.*, p. 222.
[5] *Ibid.*, p. 250.
[6] *Ibid.*, p. 181.
[7] For a discussion of this subject, see Lomax, "Self-pity in Negro Folk Song," *Nation*, vol. 105, pp. 141-45.

to his hard lot. The following expressions will make the point clear. [1]

> Bad luck in de family, sho' God, fell on me,
> Good ol' boy, jus' ain't treated right.
>
> Poor ol' boy, long ways from home,
> I'm out in dis wide worl' alone.
>
> Out in dis wide worl' to roam,
> Ain't got no place to call my home.
>
> Now my mama's dead and my sweet ol' popper too,
> An' I ain't got no one fer to carry my troubles to.
>
> If I wus to die, little girl, so far away from home,
> The folks, honey, for miles around would mourn.

Now it is apparent to any one familiar with the folk songs of various peoples that the blues type, as it has been described above, is not peculiar to the Negro, but is more or less common to all races and peoples. So far as subject matter and emotional expression are concerned, the lonesome songs of the Kentucky mountaineer, of the cowboy, of the sailor, or of any other group, are representative of the blues type. If this be so, then why was it that the Negro's song alone became the basis for a nationally popular type of song? The answer to this question is, of course, far from simple. For one thing, the whole matter of the Negro's cultural position in relation to the white man is involved. The Negro's reputation for humor and good singing is also important. Perhaps, too, the psychology of fads would have to be considered. But, speaking in terms of the qualities of the songs themselves, what is there about them to account for the superior status enjoyed by the Negro's melancholy songs?

---

[1] Illustrations are taken from *The Negro and His Songs* unless otherwise indicated.

To begin with, the Negro's peculiar use of the word "blues" in his songs was a circumstance of no mean importance.   Much more significant, however, was the music of the blues.   The blues originated, of course, with Negroes who had access to few instruments other than the banjo and the guitar.   But such music as they brought forth from these instruments to accompany their blues was suited to the indigo mood.   It was syncopated, it was full of bizarre harmonies, sudden changes of key and plaintive slurs.   It was something new to white America, and it needed only an introduction to insure its success.

But there is still another feature of the blues which is probably responsible more than any other one thing for their appeal and fascination, and that is their lack of conventionality, their naïveté of expression.   The Negro wastes no time in roundabout or stilted modes of speech.   His tale is brief, his metaphor striking, his imagery perfect, his humor plaintive.   Expressions like the following have made the blues famous.

> Looked down the road jus' far as I could see,
> Well, the band did play "Nearer, My God to Thee."

> Well, I started to leave an' I got 'way down the track;
> Got to thinkin' 'bout my woman, come a-runnin' back.

> Wish to God some ol' train would run,
> Carry me back where I came frum.

> I laid in jail, back to the wall:
> Brown skin gal cause of it all. [1]

When the first published blues appeared, the problem for the student of Negro song began to become complicated.   It is no longer possible to speak with certainty of the folk blues, so entangled are the re-

---

[1] See Perrow, "Songs and Rhymes from the South," *Journal of American Folk-Lore*, vol. 28, p. 190.

lations between them and the formal compositions. This inter-relation is itself of such interest and importance that it demands the careful attention of students of folk song. Only a few points can be touched upon in the present work, but an attempt will be made at least to indicate some of the ramifications of the subject.

There is no doubt that the first songs appearing in print under the name of blues were based directly upon actual songs already current among Negroes. [1] Soon after Handy began to issue his blues, white people as well as Negroes were singing them heartily. But a song was never sung long in its original version alone. The half-dozen stanzas of the original often grew to a hundred or more, for many singers took pride in creating new stanzas or adapting parts of other songs to the new one. Sometimes publishers would issue second and third editions, incorporating in them the best of the stanzas which had sprung up since the preceding edition. Thus, even before the phonograph became the popular instrument that it is today, the interplay between folk creations and formal compositions had become extremely complex.

In the last ten years the phonograph record has surpassed sheet music as a conveyor of blues to the public. Sheet music, however, is still important. In fact, practically every "hit" is issued in both the published and phonographed form. But the phonograph record obviously has certain advantages, and it is largely responsible for the present popularity of the blues. Most of the large phonograph companies now maintain special departments devoted to the recording

[1] See James Weldon Johnson, *The Book of American Negro Poetry*, pp. x-xiv; and Dorothy Scarborough, *On the Trail of Negro Folk-Songs*, pp. 269-70.

of "race blues." They employ Negro artists, many of whom have already earned national reputations, and they advertise extensively, expecially in the Negro press.

In spite of the extremes to which exploitation of the blues has gone in recent years, there is often an authentic folk element to be found in the present-day formal productions. Some of the phonograph artists are encouraged by their employers to sing blues of their own making. When the artist has had an intimate acquaintance with the life of his race and has grown up among the blues, so to speak, he is often able to produce a song which preserves faithfully the spirit of the folk blues. The folk productions of yesterday are likely to be found, albeit sometimes in versions scarcely recognizable, on the phonograph records of today. That this is the case is indicated by the following comparison of a few of the lines and titles of songs collected twenty years ago with lines and titles of recent popular blues songs.

Lines and Titles of Songs Collected Twenty Years Ago [1]	Lines and Titles of Recent Popular Blues
Laid in jail, back to the wall.	*Thirty days in jail with my back turned to the wall.*
Jailer, won't you put 'nother man in my stall?	*Look here, mister jailer, put another gal in my stall.*
Baby, won't you please come home?	*Baby, won't you please come home?*
Wonder where my baby stay las' night?	*Where did you stay last night?*
I got my all-night trick, baby, and you can't git in.	*I'm busy and you can't come in.*

---

[1] See *Journal of American Folk-Lore*, vol. 24; also *The Negro and His Songs*.

I'll see her when her trouble's like mine.	*I'm gonna see you when your troubles are just like mine.*
Satisfied.	*I'm satisfied.*
You may go, but this will bring you back.	*I got what it takes to bring you back.*
Joe Turner	*Joe Turner blues.*
Love, Kelly's love.	*Love, careless, love.*
I'm on my las' go-'round.	*Last go-'round blues.*

When a blues record is issued it quickly becomes the property of a million Negro workers and adventurers who never bought it and perhaps never heard it played. Sometimes they do not even know that the song is from a record. They may recognize in it parts of songs long familiar to them and think that it is just another piece which some songster has put together. Their desire to invent a different version, their skill at adapting stanzas of old favorites to the new music, and sometimes their misunderstanding of the words of the new song, result in the transformation of the song into many local variants. In other words, the folk creative process operates upon a song, the origin of which may already be mixed, and produces in turn variations that may later become the bases of other formal blues. A thorough exposition of this process would take us far beyond the limits of this volume, but the following instances are cited to illustrate generally the interplay between the folk blues and the formal blues.

Here is a specimen captured from a Negro girl in Georgia who had just returned from a trip to "Troit," Michigan.

When you see me comin'
Throw yo' woman out de do',

For you know I's no stranger,
For I's been dere once befo'.

He wrote me a letter,
Nothin' in it but a note.
I set down an' writ him,
"I ain't no billy goat."

Standin' on de platform,
Worried in both heart an' soul;
An' befo' I'd take yo' man
I'd eat grass like a Georgia mule.

I love my man
Lak I love myse'f.
If he don't have me
He won't have nobody else.

Now this song is a mixture of several popular blues.
The first stanza is from the *House Rent Blues*, and is
sung practically the same as on the phonograph record.
The second stanza is from the *Salt Water Blues* and is
like the original except for the repetition in the original
of the first two lines. The third stanza is also from
the *Salt Water Blues*, but it is a combination and
variation of two stanzas which go as follows:

Sittin' on the curbstone,
Worried in both heart an' soul;
Lower than a 'possum
Hidin' in a ground-hog hole.

I wrote my man,
"I ain't nobody's fool;
An' befo' I'd stand your talkin'
I'd eat grass like a Georgia mule."

This girl does not worry over the lack of consistent
meaning in the third stanza of her song. Furthermore,
as far as she is concerned, "soul" and "mule" rhyme
about as well as "fool" and "mule." The fourth

stanza of her song, finally, is taken from *Any Woman's Blues*, there having been, however, a slight variation in the second line. The original is:

> I love my man
> Better than I love myself;
> An' if he don't have me,
> He won't have nobody else.

Thus in a single song we have examples of the processes of borrowing, combining, changing, and misunderstanding through which formal material often goes when it gets into the hands of the common folk. The composite of four stanzas presented above has no very clear meaning in its present form, but at that it is about as coherent as any of the blues from which it was assembled.

Left Wing Gordon, whose story is told in Chapter XII, is a good study in the relation of folk song and formal blues. Left Wing's repertoire is practically unlimited, for he appears to have remembered everything that he has ever heard. One of his favorite expressions is

> You don't know my mind,
> You don't know my mind;
> When you see my laughin',
> I'm laughin' to keep from cryin'.

This comes from *You Don't Know My Mind Blues*, a popular sheet music and phonograph piece today. Left Wing sings dozens of stanzas, some evidently from the published versions, some of his own making, ending each one with "You don't know my mind," etc. Nearly all of his songs showed this sort of mixture of formal and folk material.

As an example of the misunderstanding, deliberate twisting of the words of a phonograph blues, or lapse of memory, the following instance may be cited. In the *Chain Gang Blues* this stanza occurs.

> Judge he gave me six months
> 'Cause I wouldn't go to work.
> From sunrise to sunset
> I ain't got no time to shirk.

A Southern Negro on a chain gang recently sang it thus:

> Judge he give me sentence
> 'Cause I wouldn't go to work.
> From sunrise to sunset
> I don't have no other clean shirt.

Examples of this kind might be multiplied indefinitely, but these will suffice. In the notes on the songs in the various chapters of this book will be found comments bearing upon the relation of formal blues and folk songs.

Thus it is clear that in many cases there is a complex inter-relation and interaction between the folk song and the formal production. But the tendency has been on the whole for the latter to get further and further away from folk sources. Few authors now attempt to do more than imitate certain features of the old-time blues. In order to understand more clearly the present situation, it is necessary to consider for a moment the blues as they are manufactured today.

There are at least three large phonograph companies which give special attention to Negro songs. They will be designated herein as "A," "B," and "C." The following table, compiled from data obtained from the general "race record" catalogs of these three companies, gives an idea of the importance of the blues.

Brand of Record	Total No. of Titles in Catalog	No. Religious and Classical Titles	No. Secular Titles	Titles Containing Word "Blues"	
				Number	Percentage of Secular Songs
"A"	592	34*	558	263	43
"B"	430	90†	340	154	40
"C"	298	44*	254	108	42

*No classical titles listed.　†Includes 28 classical titles.

In this table only those titles including the word "blues" have been counted as blues. If the term were expanded to include all songs which are now popularly known as blues, it would be found that upwards of seventy-five per cent of the total number of secular songs listed in the catalogs would fall in this class. The "A" catalog bears the title, *"A" Race Records— The Blue Book of Blues;* the "B" catalog follows titles like *Oh, Daddy, Brown Baby, Long Lost Mama,* etc., with the explanation, "blues song" or "blues record"; and the "C" catalog bears the title, *"C" Race Records—The Latest Blues by "C" Colored Artists.* Certainly the popular notion among both whites and Negroes now is that practically every Negro song which is not classed as a spiritual is a blues. The term is now freely applied to instrumental pieces, especially to dance music of the jazz type, and to every vocal piece which, by any stretch of the imagination, can be thought of as having a bluish cast.

A survey of the titles in the three catalogs mentioned above yields some interesting data concerning the nature of the formal blues. For one thing, there are sixty or seventy titles of the place or locality type. Southern states and cities figure prominently in this kind of blues, although the popularity of Northern localities is on the increase. The favorite states are Alabama, Georgia, Louisiana, Mississippi, Texas, and Virginia. The chief titles for these states are as follows:

ALABAMA
Alabama Blues
Birmingham Blues
Mobile Blues
Selma Bama Blues
Bama Bound Blues

GEORGIA
Atlanta Blues
Decatur Blues
Georgia Hunch
Georgia Blues

LOUISIANA
Lake Ponchartrain Blues
Lou'siana Low-down Blues
New Orleans Hop Scop Blues
New Orleans Wiggle
Shreveport Blues

MISSISSIPPI
Mississippi Blues
Ole Miss Blues
Mississippi Delta Blues

TEXAS
Dallas Blues
Houston Blues
Red River Blues
Waco Texas Blues
Seawall Special Blues

VIRGINIA
Virginia Blues
Hampton Roads Blues
Norfolk Blues

There are also, to name only a few others, *Arkansas Blues, Florida Blues, California Blues, Carolina Blues, Omaha Blues, Michigan Water Blues, Memphis Blues, Tulsa Blues, St. Louis Blues, Salt Lake City Blues, Wabash Blues,* and *Blue Grass Blues.* Finally there are foreign titles, such as *London Blues* and *West Indies Blues.* Titles, of course, are not to be taken as accurate indices of the contents of the songs. As a matter of fact, most of the songs bearing titles of the locality type really deal with the relation of man and woman.

Another feature of the formal blues is their tendency to specialize in certain slang expressions. "Sweet

mama," "sweet papa," "daddy," "jelly roll," and a few
other expressions have been thoroughly popularized
among certain classes, white and Negro, by the blues
songs. By actual count, titles containing one or
more of the words, "mama," "daddy," "papa,"
"baby," constitute twenty-five per cent of the total
number of secular titles in the catalogs referred to
above.

It is to be expected that a very large proportion of
these present-day blues (using the term now in the
broad sense as it is popularly used) deals with the
relation of man and woman. In fact, if the locality
types, most of which are based on the love relation,
and the "mama-papa" type were eliminated from the
count, there would be a mere handful left. The
following titles will give some impression of the nature
of the songs which deal with the man-woman relation. [1]

Leave My Sweet Papa Alone

I've Got a Do-right Daddy Now

Mistreated Mama

Slow Down, Sweet Papa, Mama's Catching up With You

Sweet Smellin' Mama

Black but Sweet, O God

---

[1] Any one who is acquainted with the slang and vulgarity of the lower
class Negro will suspect immediately that there are often double meanings
in titles like those listed here. Such is the case. Negro songs writers and
phonograph artists usually have had intimate acquaintance with Negro
life in all of its forms, and they have doubtless come across many a song which
was too vulgar to be put into print, but which had certain appealing qualities.
Often a melody was too striking to be allowed to escape, so the writer fitted
legitimate verses to it and, if it was at all possible, preserved the original
title. Thus it comes about that many of the popular Negro songs of today
—and white songs, too, as for that—have titles that are extremely suggestive, and are saved only by their perfectly innocuous verses. The sug-
gestiveness of the titles may also be one explanation of why these songs
have such a tremendous appeal for the common folk, black and white. It
may be that in these songs, whitewashed and masked though they be, they
recognize old friends.

How Do You Expect to Get My Lovin'?

He May Be Your Man, but He Comes to See Me Sometimes

Changeable Daddy

Go Back Where You Stayed Last Night

*How Can I Be Your Sweet "Mama" When You're "Daddy"
  to Some One Else?*

You Can Have My Man if He Comes to See You Too

That Free and Easy Papa of Mine

You Can't Do What My Last Man Did

Mistreatin' Daddy

*If I Let You Get Away With It Once You'll Do It All the
  Time*

Daddy, You've Done Put That Thing on Me

I'm Tired of Begging You to Treat Me Right

My Man Rocks Me With One Steady Roll

Do It a Long Time, Papa

No Second Handed Lovin' for Mine

I Want a Jazzy Kiss

I'm Gonna Tear Your Playhouse Down

Beale Street Mama

Big Fat Mama

Lonesome Mama

You've Got Everything a Sweet Mama Needs but Me

*If You Don't Give Me What I Want I'm Gonna Get It
  Somewhere Else*

Mama Don't Want Sweet Man Any More

If You Sheik on Your Mama

Mean Papa, Turn in Your Key

Take It, Daddy, It's All Yours

How Long, Sweet Daddy, How Long?

You Can Take My Man but You Can't Keep Him Long

Can Anybody Take Sweet Mama's Place?
You Don't Know My Mind
Baby, Wont' You Please Come Home?

Then there are innumerable miscellaneous titles and sentiments. One may have the *Poor Man Blues, Red Hot Blues, Through Train Blues, Railroad Blues, Crazy Blues, Stranger Blues, Don't Care Blues, Goin' 'Way Blues, Bleedin' Hearted Blues, Cryin' Blues, Salt Water Blues, Mountain Top Blues, Thunderstorm Blues, Sinful Blues, Basement Blues, House Rent Blues, Reckless Blues,* and even the *A to Z Blues.* Here again however, titles are misleading, for practically all songs bearing such titles really deal with the man-woman theme.

It may be worth mentioning that the majority of these formal blues are sung from the point of view of woman. A survey of titles in the "A," "B," and "C" catalogs shows that upwards of seventy-five per cent of the songs are written from the woman's point of view. Among the blues singers who have gained a more or less national recognition there is scarcely a man's name to be found.

It is doubtful whether the history of song affords a parallel to the American situation with regard to the blues. Here we have the phenomenon of a type of folk song becoming a great fad and being exploited in every conceivable form; of hundreds of blues, some of which are based directly upon folk productions, being distributed literally by the million among the American people; and the Negro's assimilation of these blues into his everyday song life. What the effects of these processes are going to be, one can only surmise. One thing is certain, however, and that is that the student of Negro song tomorrow will have to know what was on the phonograph records of today before he may dare to speak of origins.

Whether the formal blues have come to stay or not, it is impossible to tell at present. Possibly they will undergo considerable modification as the public becomes satiated and the Negro takes on more and more of the refinements of civilization. That their present form, however, is acceptable to a large section of Negro America is indicated by the fact that the combined sales of "A," "B," and "C" blues records alone amount to five or six millions annually.

The folk blues will also undergo modification, but they will always reflect Negro life in its lower strata much more accurately than the formal blues can. For it must be remembered that these folk blues were the Negro's melancholy song long before the phonograph was invented. Yet the formal songs are important. In their own way they are vastly superior to the cruder folk productions, since they have all of the advantages of the artificial over the natural. They may replace some of the simpler songs and thus dull the creative impulse of the common Negro folk to some extent, but there is every reason to suppose that there will be real folk blues as long as there are Negro toilers and adventurers whose naïveté has not been worn off by what the white man calls culture.

The plaintiveness of the blues will be encountered in most of the songs of this volume. It is present because most of the songs were collected from the class of Negro folk who are most likely to create blues. In the next chapter certain general songs of the blues type have been brought together but the note of lonesomeness and melancholy will be struck in the songs of the other chapters as well, especially in those dealing with jail and chain gang, construction camp, and the relation of man and woman.

CHAPTER III

SONGS OF THE LONESOME ROAD

THE blues *par excellence* are, of course, to be found in those songs of sorrow and disappointment and longing which center around the love relation.[1] But the song of the "po' boy long ways from home" who wanders "down that lonesome road" is rich in pathos and plaintiveness. The wanderer is not unlike the old singer who sang,

> Sometimes I hangs my head an' cries
>
> I'm po' little orphan chile in de worl'
>
> Sometimes I feel like a motherless chile
>
> Nobody knows de trouble I've had
>
> This ol' worl's been a hell to me
>
> I'm rollin' through an unfriendly worl'

Typical of the lonesome note in the present-day songs of the wanderer are the following lines:

> I'm gonna tell my mama when I git home
> How people treated me way off from home
>
> Freezin' ground wus my foldin' bed las' night
>
> Got up in the mornin', couldn't keep from cryin'
>
> My shoes all wore out
>
> My clothes done tore to pieces
>
> Trouble gonna follow me to my grave
>
> Bad luck in family, sho' God, fell on me
>
> Ain't got nuthin' to eat
>
> Sick all night on de street

---

[1] See Chapters VII and VIII for, the songs of this type. This chapter deals with more general lonesome songs.

I been mistreated all my days
Po' boy got nowhere to lay his head
Well, rock was my pillah las' night
Clothes all wet, feet on the ground
Po' boy, dey don't give me no show
Law', I'm so worried I don't know what to do
I'm gonna ketch dat train, don't know where it's from
The workhouse settin' 'way out on lonesome road
Always wanderin' about
Nowhere to lay my head
Dis po' man's life is misery
Pocketbook was empty, my heart was full of pain

In the "Annals and Blues of Left Wing Gordon" [1] will be found something of the story of one representative of all those black folk who sing down the lonesome road. Left Wing had traveled the lonesome road in at least thirty-eight states of the union. His type is legion. Here is another whose parents died before he was eight years of age. Thence to Texas, and Louisiana, across Mississippi to Georgia, then down to Florida, back through South Carolina to his home state, North Carolina. Abiding there shortly, thence to Maryland and Washington, to St. Louis, thence to Ohio, thence to New York, back to Philadelphia, across again to Ohio, then the war and camp, and armistice and more travels, with periods of "doing time." Then back again to the lonesome road.

Nowhere is self-pity in the plaintive song better expressed than in the forlorn Negro's vision of himself, the last actor in the wanderer drama, folks mourning his death, hacks in line, funeral well provided for.

---

[1] See Chapter XII.

Sometimes reflecting on his hard life, he pictures his own funeral!

> Look down po' lonesome road,
> Hacks all dead in line;
> Some give nickel, some give a dime,
> To bury dis po' body o' mine.

Perhaps he will jump into the sea or off the mountain or lay his head on a railroad track. Then folks will miss him and mourn his tragic end. He feels that he has more than his share of trouble and hard luck. Sometimes he sings that he cannot keep from crying:

> I can't keep from cryin'
>
> Look down dat lonesome road an' cry
>
> You made me weep, you made me moan
>
> Woke up in de mornin', couldn't keep from cryin'
>
> I got de blues an' can't keep from cryin'

The following songs show this note of hard luck, weeping, and self-pity:

SHIP MY PO' BODY HOME

> If I should die long way from home
> Ship my po' body home.
> Ax fer a nickel, ax fer a dime,
> Ax fer a quarter, ship my po' body home,
> Lawd, ship my po' body home.
>
> Ain't got no money,
> Ain't got nothin' to eat,
> Sick all night on de street;
> If I die long way from home
> Ship my po' body home.

PITY PO' BOY

Pity a po' boy
Stray 'way from home,
Pity a po' boy
Stray 'way from home.

If I ever gits back,
I sho' never mo' to roam;
If I ever gits back,
I sho' never mo' to roam.

I RATHER BE IN MY GRAVE

I lef' my rider standin' in back do' cryin',
"Lawd, please don't leave me behin'."

You mistreat me, you drove me from yo' do',
Good book say you got to reap what you sow.

I'm goin' 'way, Lawd, I'm goin' 'way,
I ain't comin' back, Lawd, at all.

If my mind don't change, Lawd,
If my mind don't change, I ain't comin' back.

Woke up this mornin', blues all around my bed,
Snatch up my pillow, blues all under my head.

I'm feelin' blue, mama, feel blue you know,
I feel blue all day long.

Lawd, I'm worried now, Lawd,
But I won't be worried long.

I feel like train, mama,
Ain't got no drivin' wheel.

I rather be daid in six foot o' clay,
I rather be in my grave.

THROW MYSELF DOWN IN DE SEA

Goin' up on mountain top,
Lord, goin' up on mountain top,
O Lord, goin' up on mountain top,
Throw myself down in de sea.

Throw myself down in sea,
O Lord, throw myself down in sea;
Goin' up on mountain top,
Throw myself down in sea.

Po' Nigger Got Nowhere to Go

Po' nigger got nowhere to go,
Po' nigger got nowhere to go,
Po' nigger got nowhere to go,
Nothin' but dirt all over de flo'.

Clothes am dirty rags,
Clothes am dirty rags,
Clothes am dirty rags,
Stuff in dirty bags.

Beds am ragged an' ol',
Beds am ragged an ol',
Beds am ragged an' ol',
No money to buy no mo'.

I Wish I Was Dead

Over de hill is de po' house,
Please don't let me go.
A place to sleep, somethin' to eat,
I don't ast no mo',
I don't ast no mo'.

My clothes am done tore to pieces,
My shoes am all wo' out;
Got nobody to do my patchin',
Always wanderin' about,
Always wanderin' about.

Aint' got nobody to love me,
Nowhere to lay my head.
Dis po' man's life am a misery,
Lawd, Lawd, how I wish I was dead,
Lawd, Lawd, how I wish I was dead.

Trouble All My Days [1]

Trouble, trouble,
Been had it all my days.
Trouble, trouble,
Got to mend dis nigger's ways.

Trouble, trouble,
I believe to my soul
Trouble gonna kill me dead.
Trouble, trouble.

But I's gwine away
To rid trouble off my min'.
But I's gwine away,
To rid trouble off my min'.

Fair brown, fair brown,
Who may yo' regular be?
If you got no regular,
Please take a peep at me.

Trouble, trouble,
Been had it all my day;
Believe to my soul
Trouble gonna kill me dead.

Say, look here, man,
See what you done done;
You done made me love you,
Now you tryin' to dog me 'roun'.

I Can't Keep From Cryin' [2]

I received a letter that my daddy was dead,
He wasn't dead but he was slowly dyin'.
Just to think how I love him,
I can't keep from cryin'.

I followed my daddy to the buryin' ground,
I saw the pall-bearer slowly ease him down.

---

[1] This song is very much like a popular phonograph record, *Downhearted Blues.* Cf. also *Trouble, Trouvle Blues.*
[2] A somewhat condensed version of a phonograph song, *Death Letter Blues.*

That was the last time I saw my daddy's face.
I love you, sweet daddy, but I just can't take your place.

Po' LITTLE GIRL GRIEVIN'

Po' little girl grievin',
Po' little girl grievin',
Lawdy, Lawdy, po' little girl grievin',
Po' little girl grievin'.

Little girl wid head hung down,
Little girl wid head hung down,
Lawdy, Lawdy, little girl wid head hung down,
I'm sorry for little girl wid head hung down.

Sorry yo' man,
Sorry yo' man,
Lawdy, Lawdy, sorry
Yo' man done left you.

Standin' at station weepin',
Standin' at station weepin',
Lawd, standin' at station weepin'
'Cause her man done gone.

Don't treat me lak used to,
Don't treat me lak used to,
Lawd, girl don't treat me lak used to,
Dont' treat me lak used to.

Lawd, I don't know why,
Lawd, I don't know why,
Lawdy, Lawdy, I don't know why,
Don't treat me lak used to.

It won't be long,
It won't be long,
Lawdy, Lawd, it won't be long,
Lawd, it won't be long.

The old line, "po' boy 'long way from home," is
still a favorite. In the Negro's songs and stories of
wanderings, home and father and mother are themes
of constant appeal, apparently much in contrast to the

Negro's actual home-abiding experiences. The old spirituals sang mostly of the heavenly home of dreams and ideals as opposed to the experience in which "this ol' world been a hell to me." In his wanderer song of today the Negro's wish-dream to be back home appears an equally striking contrast. Nowhere in the workaday songs is childlike and wishful yearning so marked as in these constant songs of homesickness and of the desire for something that is not.

Always accompanying the singer's dreams of home is his contrasting forlorn condition in the present hour. It would be difficult to find better description of situations than that in which he pictures himself as tired and forsaken on the lonesome road. Parts of this picture may be gathered from the following lines taken here and there from his songs:

> Take, oh, take me, take me back home
>
> My sister's cryin' back home
>
> If I die long way from home
>
> My home ain't here an' I ain't got to stay
>
> O Lord, captain, won't you let me go home
>
> Daddy sick, mammy dead,
> Goin' back South, dat's where I'm bound.
>
> Every mail day I gits letter from my mother,
> Sayin', "Son, son, come home."
>
> I'm one hundred miles from home
> An' I can't go home this way.
>
> I didn't have no ready-made money,
> I couldn't go home.
>
> A place to sleep, something to eat,
> I don't ast no mo'.
>
> Look down dat lonesome road an' cry

A variety of songs of home or home-folk, of surcease from work, will be found wherever Negroes
sing. This fact is recognized by the publishers of
blues when they advertise, "These blues will make
every Negro want to hurry back home." The plaintive longing for home, alongside expressions of weeping
and self-pity, is the theme of most of the following
songs of the road:

I'm Goin' Home, Buddie

All 'round the mountain, Buddie,
So chilly and cold, Buddie,
So chilly and cold, Buddie,
But I'm goin' home, Buddie, I'm goin' home.

Take this hammer, Buddie,
Carry it to the boss, Buddie,
Carry it to the boss, Buddie,
Tell him I gone home, Buddie, I gone home.

I got a wife, Buddie,
With two little children, Buddie,
With two little children, Buddie,
Tell 'em I'm comin' home, Buddie, I'm comin' home.

That Ol' Letter

That ol' letter,
Read about dyin';
Boy, did you ever,
Think about dyin'?
Then I can't read it
Now for cryin',
Tears run down,
Lawd, Lawd, tears run down.

Po' Homeless Boy

In de evenin' de sun am low,
In de evenin' de sun am low,
In de evenin' de sun am low,

Dis po' homeless boy got nowhere to go,
Dis po' homeless boy got nowhere to go,
Nowhere to go.

Daddy sick, mammy daid,
Daddy sick, mammy daid,
Po' boy got nowhere to lay his haid,
Po' boy got nowhere to lay his haid,
Lay his haid.

Clothes all wo', feet on de groun',
Clothes all wo', feet on de groun',
Goin' back down South, dat's where I's boun',
Goin' back down South, dat's where I's boun',
Where I's boun'.

Home in a two-room shack,
Home in a two-room shack,
Home in a two-room shack,
Cook in de fire, pipe in de crack,
Cook in de fire, pipe in de crack,
Pipe in de crack.

TAKE ME BACK HOME

Take me, oh, take me,
Take me back home.

My mammy's weepin', daddy's sleepin',
In de ol' grave yard.

Take me, oh, take me,
Take me back home.

PLEASE, MR. CONDUCTOR

When I left home mother was ill,
And she needed the doctor's care,
That's the reason I came to the city,
I'll pay you my fare next time.

Please, Mr. Conductor,
Don't put me off this train.
The best friend I have in this world
Is waiting for me in pain.

Captain, I Wanta Go Home

When I call on captain, Lawd, Lawd,
He ast me what I need.

Captain, captain, I tol' captain,
Lawd, I wanta go back home.

He tol' me, Lawd, why you want to go home, Shine?
Say you got to make your time.

Captain call me 'bout half pas' fo',
Captain, Lawd, I wouldn't go.

Want me to go in kitchen,
Draw water, make fire.

Captain, captain, what make you call me so soon?
Poor Shine, Lawd, captain, wish I was home.

I went out on road
Wid pick and shovel, too.

I pick a lick or two,
Captain, can't I go back home?

Captain, captain, won't you take me,
Lawd, Lawd, captain, won't you take me back?

My home ain't here, captain,
An' I ain't got to stay.

O Lawd, captain, captain, Lawd,
Won't you let me go home?

Will I Git Back Home?

Law', I do wonder,
Law', I do wonder,
Law', I do wonder,
Will I git back home, huh?
Will I git back home, huh?

Well cuckoo, cuckoo,
Keep on hollerin',
An' mus' be day, Law',
Mus' be day.

Well whistle, whistle,
Keep on blowin',
An' time ain't long,
Uhuh, time ain't long.

LAWD, LAWD, I'M ON MY WAY

Aint' had nothin' to eat,
Ain't had nowhere to sleep,
Freezin' ground wus my foldin' bed,
But I'm on my way,
O Lawd, I'm on my way.

What makes you hold yo' head so high?
Any way you hold yo' head,
That's way you gonna die,
That's way you gonna die.

I sho' don't want to go,
But I'm goin' up country
Singin' nothin' but you;
I'm goin' up country,
Singin' nothin' but you.

GOIN' DOWN DAT LONESOME ROAD [1]

Goin' down dat lonesome road,
Oh, goin' down dat lonesome road,
An' I won't be treated this-a way.
Springs on my bed done broken down,
An' I ain't got nowhere to lay my head.

Now my mamma's dead an' my papa, too,
An' it left me alone wid you.
An' you cause me to weep an' you cause me to moan,
An' you cause me to leave my happy home.

Longest train I ever saw
Was nineteen coaches long.
Darlin' what have I done to you?
What makes you treat me so?
An' I won't be treated this-a way.

---

[1] For the music of this song, see Chapter XIV. A song of this name has been found in the Kentucky mountains, and a phonograph record (*Lonesome Road Blues*) based on it has recently appeared. Cf. also *The Lonesome Road* in Miss Scarborough's *On the Trail of Negro Folk-Songs*, p. 73.

CHAPTER IV

BAD MAN BALLADS AND JAMBOREE

THERE is this fortunate circumstance which contributes to the completeness and vividness of the Negro portraits as found in workaday songs: the whole picture is often epitomized in each of several characters or types of singers and their songs. Thus the picture may be viewed from all sides and from different angles, with such leisure and repetition as will insure accurate impressions. One of these types is the "po' boy long way from home" singing down "that lonesome road," as represented in the previous chapter. Whether in his ordinary daily task, or on his pilgrimages afar, or in the meshes of the law, this singer approaches perfection in the delineation of his type. Another type is that to be found in the story of Left Wing Gordon as presented in Chapter XII, and of John Henry in Chapter XIII. Likewise, the songs of jail and chain gang, the songs of women and love, and the specialized road songs all embody that fine quality of full and complete reflection of the folk spirit in the Negro's workaday life and experience.

There is perhaps no type, however, which comes more nearly summarizing certain situations, experiences, and backgrounds than the Negro "bad man," whose story will make an heroic tale of considerable proportions. In many ways the "bad man from bad man's land" is a favorite. He is eulogized by the youngsters and sung by the worker by the side of the road. One preacher even described Christ as a man who would "stand no foolin' wid." "Jesus such great man, no one lak him. Lord, he could pop lion's head

off jes' lak he wus fryin'-size chicken an' could take
piece o' mountain top and throw it across the world."
And as for that other bad man, "Nicotemus," why
Jesus, when he got through with him, had him following
behind a donkey like any other slave. [1] There was
that other young Negro who "was no comfort to
preacher, but was a hawk like pizen. Mens like him
and wimmin belonged to him wid his winnin' ways."
In a previous volume [2] we pointed out some of the
characteristic experiences and modes of the Negro
bum, "bully of this town," Railroad Bill, Stagolee,
Brady, and the others, of twenty years ago. Since
that time the tribe has apparently not diminished and
flourishes well in the atmosphere of modern life,
migration, and the changing conditions of race re-
lations. Of the statistical and environmental aspects
of the Negro criminal much will be reported in another
study. [3] In this chapter we are concerned with the
portrait of a type, perhaps inexorably drawn into the
maelstrom of his day and turned into an inevitable
product. He is no less an artist than the wanderer,
the "travelin' man," or Left Wing Gordon. He is the
personification of badness mixed with humor, of the
bad man and the champion of exploits. We have
already referred to the Negro who "wus so mean wus
skeered of hisself," competitor to that other one
whose

> . . . eyes wus red an' his gums wus blue,
> 'Cause he wus a nigger right through and through.

There were still other companions to these in Slippery
Jim, Slewfoot Pete, and Ann-Eliza Stone, "mean wid

---

[1] Cited by Dr. E. C. L. Adams of Columbia, S. C.
[2] *The Negro and His Songs*, page 164 seq.
[3] A study of Negro crime directed by J. F. Steiner, for the Institute
for Research in Social Science, at the University of North Carolina.

her habbits on" and breaking up the "jamboree." [1]
A common phrase, indeed, threatened always to "break
up dis jamboree" in exchange for slighting one's
"repertation."

Many are the bad men, and vivid the descriptions.
Said one, "Lawd, cap'n, take me till tomorrow night
to tell 'bout dat boy. Eve'ybody skeered uv him.
John Wilson jes nachelly bully, double j'inted, awful
big man, didn't fear 'roun' nobody. Would break
up ev'y do he 'tended. Go to picnic, take all money
off'n table. Couldn't do nothin' wid him. Seen
feller shoot at him nine times once an' didn't do nothin
to him, an' he run an' caught up wid feller an' bit
chunk meat out o' his back, . . . but one man
got him wid britch loader an' stop 'im from suckin'
eggs."

We have found no black bad-man ballads superior to
the old ones, *Railroad Bill, Stagolee, That Bully of
this Town, Desperado Bill, Eddy Jones, Joe Turner,
Brady,* [2] and the others. And yet, the current stories
sung on the road are more accurate portrayals of actual
characters and experiences, and perhaps less finished
songs, less formal rhyme. Take *Lazarus,* for instance,
a hard luck story, portraying something of Negro
sympathy, burial custom, general reaction. Here is a
character more to be pitied than censured, according
to his companions. Listen to three pick-and-shovel
men, tracing "po' Lazarus" from the work camp where
he, poor foolish fellow, robbed the commissary camp
and then took to his heels. Thence between the
mountains where the high sheriff shot him down, back
to the camp and burying ground, with mother, wife,

---

[1] See Swan and Abbot, in *Eight Negro Songs,* New York, 1923.
[2] *The Negro and His Songs,* pages 196-212.

brothers, sisters, comrades weeping, attending the funeral, where they "put po' Lazarus away at half pas' nine."

BAD MAN LAZARUS

Oh, bad man Lazarus,
Oh, bad man Lazarus,
He broke in de commissary,
Lawd, he broke in de commissary.

He been paid off,
He been paid off,
Lawd, Lawd, Lawd,
He been paid off.

Commissary man,
Commissary man,
He jump out commissary window,
Lawd, he jump out commissary window.

Startin' an' fall,
O Lawd, Lawd, Lawd,
Commissary man startin' an' he fall,
O Lawd, Lawd, Lawd.

Commissary man swore out,
Lawd, commissary man swore out,
Lawd, commissary man swore out
Warrant for Lazarus.

O bring him back,
Lawd, bring him back,
O Lawd, Lawd, Lawd,
Bring Lazarus back.

They began to wonder,
Lawd, they began to wonder,
Lawd, they began to wonder
Where Lazarus gone.

Where in world,
Lawd, where in world,
Lawd, where in world
Will they find him?

Well, I don't know,
I don't know,
Well, Lawd, Lawd,
Well, I don't know.

Well, the sheriff spied po' Lazarus,
Well, the sheriff spied po' Lazarus,
Lawd, sheriff spied po' Lazarus
Way between Bald Mountain.

They blowed him down,
Well, they blowed him down,
Well, Lawd, Lawd,
They blowed him down.

They shot po' Lazarus,
Lawd, they shot po' Lazarus,
Lawd, they shot po' Lazarus
With great big number,

Well, forty-five,
Lawd, great big forty-five,
Lawd, forty-five,
Turn him roun'.

They brought po' Lazarus,
And they brought po' Lazarus,
Lawd, they brought po' Lazarus
Back to the shanty.

Brought him to de number nine,
Lawd, brought him to number nine,
Lawd, they brought him to the number nine,
Lawd, they brought po' Lazarus to number nine.

Ol' friend Lazarus say,
Lawd, old friend Lazarus say,
Lawd, old friend Lazarus say,
"Give me cool drink of water.

"Befo' I die
Good Lawd, 'fo' I die,
Give me cool drink of water,
Lawd, 'fo' I die."

Lazarus' mother say,
Lawd, Lazarus' mother say,
"Nobody know trouble
I had with him,

"Since daddy died,
Lawd, since daddy been dead,
Nobody know the trouble I had
Since daddy been dead."

They goin' bury po' Lazarus,
Lawd, they goin' bury ol' Lazarus,
They goin' bury po' Lazarus
In the mine.

At half pas' nine, O Lawd,
Good Lawd, Lawd, Lawd,
Goin' bury po' Lazarus
At half pas' nine.

Me an' my buddy,
Lawd, me an' my buddy,
We goin' over to bury him,
Half pas' nine.

Half pas' nine,
O Lawd, Lawd, half pas' nine,
We goin' over to bury him,
Half pas' nine.

Lazarus' mother say,
"Look over yonder,
How dey treatin' po' Lazarus,
Lawd, Lawd, Lawd."

They puttin' him away,
Lawd, they puttin' him away,
Lawd, they puttin' Lazarus away,
Half pas' nine.

It would be difficult to find a scene and setting more appealing than this ballad being sung by a group of workingmen in unison, with remarkable harmony, fine voices, inimitable manner. "Doesn't this singing hinder you in your work?" we asked one of the pick-and-shovel men, just to see what type of reply he would make. With first a slow look of surprise, then a sort of pity for the man who would ask such a question, then a "Lawdy-Lawd-Cap'n" outburst of laughter, "Cap'n dat's whut makes us work so much better, an' it nuthin' else but." And one of the group acted the part of the "shouter" very much like the hearers in the church. He would sing a while, then dig away in silence, then burst out with some exhorter's exclamation about the song, giving zest to the singing, contrast to the imagery, authority to the story. Once as the singers recorded the shooting of Lazarus, he shouted, "Yes, yes, Lawd, Lawd, I seed 'em, I wus dere"; and again when they sang of his mother weeping, "Yes, Lawd, I wus right dere when she come a-runnin'. I know it's true." Taken all in all, the sorrowful story of Lazarus, with its painstaking sequence and its melody as sung on this occasion, it is doubtful if ever Negro spiritual surpassed it in beauty and poignancy.

The above version was heard at Danielsville, Georgia. A similar but shorter one, current in North Carolina, is called *Billy Bob Russell*. "Reason why dey calls it dat is Billy Bob Russell an' Lazarus been buddies for years, pretty mean boys til dey gits grown. Billy Bob Russell, he's from Georgia an' I think Lazarus act sorta like robber or highway robber or somethin', follow road camp all time." [1]

---

[1] Other Negroes affirm that Billy Bob Russell was a white man, a Georgia construction foreman and a very noted one.

BILLY BOB RUSSELL

Cap'n tol' high sheriff,
"Go an' bring me Lazarus,
Bring him dead or alive,
Lawd, bring him dead or alive."

Eve'ybody wonder
Where in world dey would find him,
Then I don't know,
Cap'n, I don't know.

Lazarus tol' high sheriff,
He had never been 'rested
By no one man,
Lawd, Lawd, by no one man.

Then they found po' Lazarus
In between two mountains,
Wid his head hung down,
Lawd, Lawd, wid his head hung down.

Shoot po' Lazarus,
Carried him over to shanty,
Lawd, shoot po' Lazarus,
Carried him over to shanty.

Lazarus' sister she run
An' tol' her mother
That Lazarus wus dead,
Lawd, Lazarus wus dead.

Then Lazarus tol' high sheriff,
"Please turn me over
On my wounded side,
Lawd, on my wounded side."

Lazarus tol' high sheriff,
"Please give me drink water
Jes' befo' I die,
Lawd, jes' befo' I die."

Lazarus' mother,
She laid down her sewin',
She wus thinkin' bout trouble
She had had wid Lazarus.

In contrast to the more finished rhyming stanzas of
Railroad Bill and the earlier heroic epics, note the
simple, vivid ballad-in-the-making type of unrhymed
song so common as a type of pick-and-shovel melody.
Note the accuracy of the picture, its trueness to actual
workaday experience, the phrase description. Such
a song in the making and in the rendering defies
description or competition as a folk-mirror. Differing
somewhat and yet of the same general sort of charac-
terization is the current story of Dupree, versions of
which have been taken from Asheville, North Carolina,
and various other places in Georgia and North Carolina.
One of the most interesting aspects of this Dupree
song is that it may be compared with the Atlanta
ballad of the white *Frank Dupree* as popularly sung
on the phonograph records. The story of the white
culprit warns his young friends in the usual way and
asks them to meet him in heaven. His crime was,
first, snatching a diamond ring for his sweetheart,
then shooting the policeman to death, then fleeing
but coming back because he could not stay away from
his "Betty." There is little similarity of expression
between the white version and the Negro one. Here
is the more finished of the Negro songs.

Dupree

Dupree was a bandit,
He was so brave and bol',
He stoled a diamond ring
For some of Betty's jelly roll.

Betty tol' Dupree,
"I want a diamond ring."
Dupree tol' Betty,
"I'll give you anything."

"Michigan water
Taste like cherry wine, [1]
The reason I know:
Betty drink it all the time.

"I'm going away
To the end of the railroad track.
Nothing but sweet Betty
Can bring me back."

Dupree tol' the lawyer,
"Clear me if you can,
For I have money to back me,
Sure as I'm a man."

The lawyer tol' Dupree,
"You are a very brave man,
But I think you will
Go to jail and hang."

Dupree tol' the judge,
"I am not so brave and bol',
But all I wanted
Was Betty's jelly roll."

The judge tol' Dupree,
"Jelly roll's gonna be your ruin."
"No, no, judge, for that is
What I've done quit doin'."

The judge tol' Dupree,
"I believe you quit too late,
Because it is
Already your fate."

In striking contrast to the *Dupree* just given is one
sung by a young Negro who had been in the chain gang

---

[1] See phonograph record, *Michigan Water Blues.*

a number of times and whose major repertoire consisted of the plaintive chain gang songs. Here the singer has translated the version into his own vernacular, varying lines, eschewing rhyme, carrying his story through the regular channels of the prison type. The lines are given exactly as sung, repetitions and irregularities constituting their chief distinction. And yet something of the same story runs through it. It is perhaps a little nearer the Atlanta version, and the singer adds still another interpretation that Dupree and Betty had quarreled and as a result Dupree had killed her and hidden her body in the sawdust. An interesting local color is that Dupree was sent to Milledgeville, Georgia, where as a matter of fact is situated the combined state prison and hospital. Here, then, is the song with its mixed imagery and reflection of a certain mentality.

Dupree Tol' Betty

Betty tol' Dupree
She want a diamond ring;
Betty tol' Dupree
She want a diamond ring.
Dupree tol' Betty,
Gonna pawn his watch an' chain;
Dupree tol' Betty,
Gonna pawn his watch an' chain.

Dupree left here cold in han',
Dupree left here cold in han',
But when he git back to Georgia,
He was wrapped up all in chains.

Dupree tol' Betty,
"Gonna git that diamond ring."
Betty tol' Dupree,
"If you stay in love with me,

Hurry an' git that diamond ring;
If you stay in love with me,
Hurry an' git that diamond ring."

Dupree tol' Betty,
He git that diamond ring;
Dupree tol' Betty,
He git that diamond ring,
He went to the pawnshop
An' snatched the diamond ring,
He went to the pawnshop
An' snatched the diamond ring.

High-sheriff come git Dupree,
Took him in the jail.
Lawd, jail keeper come and git Dupree,
Took him to the jail.
Lawd, jail keeper took Dupree
An' put him in his cell,
Lawd, jail keeper took Dupree
An' put him in his cell.

Dupree ask the sheriff
What he had done,
Lawd, Dupree ask the sheriff
What he had done.
Sheriff tol' him
He had snatched diamond ring,
Sheriff told him
He had snatched diamond ring.

Dupree say he ain't killed no man.
Jailer tol' him take it easy,
'Cause he done snatched the diamond ring,
'Cause he done snatched the diamond ring.
He say, "I aint got no case 'gainst you
But I bound to put you in jail."
He say, "I aint got no case 'gainst you
But I bound to put you in jail."

Dupree laid in jail
So long they tried to hang him;
They tried to take him to court

An' taken him back again,
Judge give him the same old sentence,
Lawd, judge give him the same old sentence.

Say, "Dupree you kill that po' little girl
An' hid her in the sawdust.
Dupree, we got hangin' for you,
Sorry, Dupree, we got to hang po' you."

They try to take him to Milledgeville,
Lawd, tried to take him to Milledgeville,
Put him in a orphans' home,
Lawd, to keep him out of jail.

A popular bad man song of many versions is the
Travelin' Man. No one has ever outdistanced him.
A long story, rapidly moving, miraculously achieving,
triumphantly ending, it represents jazz song, phonograph record, banjo ballad, quartet favorite, although
it is not easy to capture. Three versions have been
found in the actual singing, one by a quartet which
came to Dayton, Tennessee, to help entertain the
evolution mongers; another by Kid Ellis, of Spartan-
burg, South Carolina, himself a professed traveling
man; a third by a North Carolina Negro youth who
had, however, migrated to Pennsylvania and returned after traveling in seven or eight other states
of the union. The South Carolina version, which is
given here, is of the *Ain't Gonna Rain No Mo'*
type of vaudeville and ballad mixture.

TRAVELIN' MAN

Now I jus' wanna tell you 'bout travelin' man,
His home was in Tennessee;
He made a livin' stealin' chickens
An' anything he could see.

Chorus:

He was a travelin' man,
He certainly was a travelin' man,

He was mos' travelin' man
That ever was in this lan'.

And when the law got after that coon,
He certainly would get on the road.
An' if a train pass, no matter how fas',
He certainly would get on boa'd.

He was a travelin' man,
Was seen for miles aroun',
He never got caught, an' never give up
Until the police shot him down.

The police shot him with a rifle,
An' the bullet went through his head,
The people came for miles aroun'
To see if he was dead.

They sent down South for his mother,
She was grieved and moved with tears,
Then she open the coffin to see her son,
An' the fool had disappeared.

The police got in an auto
An' started to chase that coon,
They run him from six in the mornin'
Till seven that afternoon.

The coon ran so bloomin' fast
That fire come from his heels;
He scorched the cotton an' burnt the corn
An' cut a road through the farmer's fields.

The coon went to the spring one day
To get a pail of water;
The distance he had to go
Was two miles and a quarter.

He got there an' started back,
But he stumbled an' fell down;
He went to the house and got another pail,
An' caught the water 'fore it hit the ground.

The coon stole a thousand dollars,
Was in broad open day time.

I ast the coon if he wa'n't ashame
To commit such an awful crime.

They put the coon on the gallows
An' told him he would die;
He crossed his legs an' winked his eye
And sailed up in the sky.

The coon got on the Titanic
An' started up the ocean blue,
But when he saw the iceberg,
Right overboa'd he flew.

The white folks standin' on the deck,
Said "Coon, you are a fool."
But 'bout three minutes after that
He was shootin' craps in Liverpool.

For the rest of this picture of the bad man the simple presentation of songs and fragments in sufficient numbers to illustrate main types will suffice. His name is legion, and he ranks all the way from the "polish man" to the "boll-weevil nigger," much despised of the common man of the better sort. Bad men come into peaceful and industrious communities and disturb the peace. They flow in from other states to add to the number of offenders, yet in spite of their numbers and character, the church throng, the picnic, the funeral and other social occasions seem to have much fewer murders and fracases than formerly. If the bad man can be turned into song and verse, with the picture of adventure and romance becoming more and more mythical, the Negro will profit by the evolution. For the present, however, here are samples of the portrayals most commonly sung, with apologies to all improvisators, minstrel artists, and white-folk imitators of Negro verse.

BOLIN JONES

Bolin Jones wuz
A man of might,
He worked all day
And he fit all night.

O Lawsy, Lawsy,
He's a rough nigger,
Han' to his hip,
Fingers on de trigger.

Lay 'em low,
Lay 'em low,
When Bolin's 'round,
Mind whar you go.

ROSCOE BILL

I'm de rowdy from over de hill,
I'm de rowdy called Roscoe Bill,
Roscoe Bill, Roscoe Bill,
When I shoots I'm boun' to kill.

I'm Roscoe Bill
Dat never gits skeered,
Goes frum shack to shack,
Tries de udder man's bed.

I'm Roscoe Bill,
De man of might,
Plum tickled to death
When I raise a fight.

I'm Roscoe Bill
Dat de women all foller.
Takes what dey got,
Den steals deir dollar.

LAYIN' LOW

Layin' low, never know
When de cops about.
Shootin' crap on my gal's lap,
I've got to go my route.

Layin' low, never know,
When de p'liceman's walkin' about,
Walkin' in, stalkin' about,
Dat p'liceman's walkin' about.

Don't Fool Wid Me

Dark town alley's too small a place
For me and that cop to have a fair race.

I lay low till de night am dark,
Den dis here nigger is out for a lark.

Han's up, nigger, don't fool wid me,
I put nigger whar he ought-a be.

Creepin' 'Roun'

Work in de mornin',
In de evenin' I sleep.
When de dark comes, Lawd,
Dis nigger got to creep.

Chorus:

Creepin' 'roun',
Creepin' in,
Creepin' everywhere
A creeper's been.

Eats in de mornin',
In de evenin' I looks 'roun'.
When de dark comes, Lawd,
A chocolate gal I've foun'.

Shootin' Bill

Dere's a nigger on my track,
Dere's a nigger on my track,
Dere's a nigger on my track,
Let de undertaker take him back.

I'm a man shoots de two-gun fire,
I'm a man shoots de two-gun fire,
I'm a man shoots de two-gun fire,
I'se got a gal who's a two-faced liar.

When I shoots, I shoots to kill,
When I shoots, I shoots to kill,
When I shoots, I shoots to kill,
Dat's why dey fears Shootin' Bill!

I Am Ready For de Fight

When at night I makes my bed,
When at night I makes my bed,
When at night I makes my bed,
Puts my feets up to de head.

If dey hunts me in de night,
If dey hunts me in de night,
If dey hunts me in de night,
I am ready fer de fight.

I sleeps wid one year out,
I sleeps wid one year out,
I sleeps wid one year out,
Got to know when dem rounders 'bout.

Up an' down dis worl',
Up an' down dis worl',
Up an' down dis worl',
Lookin' fer dat tattlin' gal.

Slim Jim From Dark-town Alley

Slim Jim wus a chocolate drop,
Slim Jim wus a chocolate drop,
Slim Jim wus a chocolate drop
From dark-town alley.

Slim Jim drapped down a cop,
Slim Jim drapped down a cop,
Slim Jim drapped down a cop
In dark-town alley.

Hy Jim, hey Jim, we got you at las',
Hy Jim, hey Jim, we got you at las',
Hy Jim, hey Jim, we got you at las'
In dark-town alley.

De jails kotch him at las', dat chocolate drop,
De jails kotch him at las', dat chocolate drop,
De jails kotch him at las', dat chocolate drop
From dark-town al-ley.

Dem bars wus strong, but Chocolate melted away,
Dem bars wus strong, but Chocolate melted away,
Dem bars wus strong, but Chocolate melted away,
Back to dark-town alley.

I'm a Natural-bo'n Ram'ler

I'm a natural-bo'n ram'ler,
I'm a natural-bo'n ram'ler,
I'm a natural-bo'n ram'ler,
An' it ain't no lie.

I travels about on Monday night,
I travels about when de moon is bright.
I travels about on Tuesday, too,
I travels about when got nuthin' else to do.

I travels about on Wednesday mo'n,
Been travelin' ever since I been bo'n,
On Thurs' I rambles 'round de town,
Dey aint no Jane kin hol' me down.

Friday ketches me wid my foot in my han',
I'm de out-derndest traveler of any man.
Saturday's de day I rambles fo' sumpin to eat,
An' Sunday de day dis ram'ler sleeps.

I'm de Hot Stuff Man

I'm de hot stuff man
Frum de devil's lan'.
Go on, nigger,
Don't you try to buck me,
I'm de hot stuff man
Frum de devil's lan'.
I'm a greasy streak o' lightnin',
Don't you see?
Don't you see?
Don't you see?

I can cuss, I can cut,
I can shoot a nigger up.
Go on, nigger,
Don't you try to buck me,
I'm de fas'est man,
Can clean up de lan'.
I'm a greasy streak o' lightnin',
Can't you see?
I'm a greasy streak o' lightin',
Can't you see?

Reuben [1]

Dat you, Reuben?
Dat you, Reuben?
Den dey laid ol' Reuben down so low.

Say ol' Reuben had a wife,
He's in trouble all his life.
Den dey lay Reuben down so low.

Dat you Reuben?
Dat you Reuben?
Den dey laid Reuben down so low.

Says ol' Reuben mus' go back,
When he pawn his watch an' hack.
Den dey laid Reuben down so low.

Says ol' Reuben mus' be dead,
When he laid upon his bed.
Den dey laid Reuben down so low.

Dat you Reuben?
Dat you Reuben?
Den dey laid Reuben down so low.

Bloodhoun' on My Track

Bloodhoun' from Macon right on my track,
Right on my track, right on my track.
Bloodhoun' from Macon right on my track,
Wonder who gonna stan' my bon'?

---

[1] We are told that this song is common among the whites of Western
North Carolina.

Buffalo Bill

I'm de bad nigger,
If you wants to know;
Look at dem rounders
In de cemetery row.
Shoot, nigger,
Shoot to kill,
Who's you foolin' wid?
My Buffalo Bill?

Buffalo Bill
Wus a man of might,
Always wore his britches
Two sizes too tight.
Split 'em nigger,
Ride 'em on a rail;
I've got de mon to
Pay yo' bail.

Dat Leadin' Houn'

Dere's a creeper hangin' 'roun',
I'm gwiner git 'im I be boun'.
Den dey put dat feller in de groun'
An' I be listenin' fer dat houn',
Dat leadin' houn'.

All aroun' here,
All aroun' here,
What does I keer?
Listenin' fer dat leadin' houn'.

Steal in home middle o' de night,
Give dem folksies sich a fright.
Say, "Feed me, woman, treat me right,"
But she send fer de sheriff
An' de leadin' houn'.

Outrun Dat Cop

Hi lee, hi lo, happy on de way,
Hi lee, hi lo, outrun dat cop today.
Hi lee, hi lo, watch his shirt-tail fly,
Hi lee, hi lo, 'splain to you by and by.

Don't You Hear?

Don't you hear dat shakin' noise?
Don't you hear dat creepin' 'roun'?
Don't you hear dat stefly walkin'?
Dat's dat man I laid down, laid down.

Can't you hear dem bones a-shakin'?
Can't you hear dem dead man's moan?
Can't you see dem dead man's sperrits?
Can't you see dat man ain't gone?

I's a Natural-bo'n Eastman

I's a natural-bo'n eastman,
An' a cracker jack,
I's a natural-bo'n eastman
An' a cracker jack,
On de road again,
On de road again.

I Steal Dat Corn

I steal dat corn
From de white man's barn,
Den I slips aroun',
Tells a yarn,
An' sells it back again.

I steal dem chickens
From de white man's yard,
Den I tells dat man
I's workin' hard,
An' I sells 'em back again.

I steal de melons
From his patch,
It takes a smarter man dan him
Fer ter ketch,
An' I sells 'em back again.

I'M DE ROUGH STUFF

I'm de rough stuff of dark-town alley,
I'm de man dey hates to see.
I'm de rough stuff of dis alley,
But de womens all falls for me:

Lawd, Lawd, how dey hates me!
Lawd, Lawd, how dey swear!
Lawd, Lawd, how dey hates me!
Lawd, Lawd, what-a mo' do I care?

I AIN'T DONE NOTHIN'

Went up to 'Lanta,
Who should I meet?
Forty-leben blue coats
Comin' down de street,
Forty-leben blue coats
Comin' down de street.
I ain't done nothin',
What dey follerin' after me?
I ain't done nothin,
Can't dey let me be?

WHEN HE GRIN

His head was big an' nappy,
An' ashy wus his skin,
But good God-a'mighty, man,
You forget it when he grin.

His nose wus long an' p'inted,
His eyes wus full o' sin,
But good God-a'mighty, man,
You forget it when he grin.

His foots wus long an' bony,
An' skinny wus his shin,
But good God-a'mighty, man,
You forget it when he grin.

He'd fight ten,
He could sin, always win,
But good God-a'mighty, man,
You forget it when he grin.

SHOT MY PISTOL IN THE HEART O' TOWN [1]

O Lawd,
Shot my pistol
In the heart o' town.
Lawd, the big chief hollered,
"Doncha blow me down."

O Lawd,
Which a-way
Did the po' gal go?
She lef' here runnin',
Is all I know.

O Lawd,
Which a-way
Do the Red River run?
Lawd, it run east and west
Like the risin' sun.

Black gal hollered,
Like to scared my brown to death.
If I hadn't had my pistol
I'd a-run myself.

O Lawd,
Jes' two cards
In the deck I love
Lawd, the Jack o' Diamonds
An' the Ace o' Clubs.

O Lawd,
Stopped here to play
Jes' one mo' game.
Lawd, Jack o' Diamonds
Petered on my han'.

---

[1] For music see Chapter XIV.

CHAPTER V

SONGS OF JAIL, CHAIN GANG, AND POLICEMEN

Not all Negro "bad men" achieve an abiding place in jail or chain gang. Not all Negroes in jail or chain gang are "bad men"—not by long odds. And yet the prison population of the South contains abundant representations of both major and minor Negro offenders, although the indications are that the ratio of Negroes to whites is decreasing rapidly. And if one wishes to obtain anything like an adequate or accurate picture of the workaday Negro he will surely find much of his best setting in the chain gang, prison, or in the situations of the ever-fleeing fugitive from "chain-gang houn'," high sheriff or policeman. "I ain't free, Lawd, I ain't free," sings the prisoner who bemoans the bad luck in which he had "nobody to pay my fine." Never did the old spiritual, as in "Go down, Moses, tell ol' Pharaoh, let my people go," express more determined call for freedom than the Negro singer behind the bars. Yet the Negro prisoner combines admirable humor with his wailing song:

I Ain't Free

De rabbit in de briar patch,
De squirrel in de tree,
Would love to go huntin',
But I ain't free,
But I ain't free,
But I ain't free,
Would love to go huntin',
But I ain't free, ain't free.

De rooster's in de hen house,
De hen in de patch,
I love to go shootin'
At a ol' shootin' match;
But I ain't free,
But I ain't free,
But I ain't free,
At a ol' shootin' match,
But I ain't free, ain't free.

Ol' woman in de kitchen,
My sweetie hangin' 'roun',
'Nudder man gonna git 'er,
I sho' be boun',
'Cause I ain't free,
'Cause I ain't free,
'Cause I ain't free,
'Nudder man 'll git 'er,
'Cause I ain't free, ain't free.

Dig in de road band,
Dig in de ditch,
Chain gang got me,
An' de boss got de switch
I ain't free,
I ain't free,
I ain't free,
Chain gang got me,
An' I ain't free, ain't free.

This chapter makes no approach to the study of the Negro criminal. That will be done in the scientific inquiries which are now being made at length and in later studies of the Negro bad man. What the chapter attempts is simply to give further pictures of the Negro workaday singer as he is found behind prison bars, or with ball and chain, or in humorous workaday retrospect or prospect of experiences what time he pays the penalty for his misdoings. For these prison and road songs, policeman and sheriff epics, jail and chain gang ballads constitute an eloquent cross-section of the whole field of Negro songs. Many are sung even as the ordinary work songs; others are improvised and varied. One may listen to high-pitched voices, plaintive and wailing, until the haunting melody will abide for days. The prisoners sing of every known experience from childhood and home to "hard luck in the family, sho' God, fell on me." One youngster about twenty-one years of age, periodic offender with experience on the chain gang and in jail, sang more than one hundred songs or fragments and the end was not yet. They cannot be described; selections are not representative. And yet, listen for a while:

Jail House Wail

The jail's on fire, Lawd,
The stockade's burnin' down.

Well, they ain't got nowhere,
Lawd, to put the prisoners now.

Taken prisoners out o' jail, Lawd,
Carried 'em to county road.

Say, I ruther be in chain gang
Than be in jail all time.

Say, jailer keep you bound down,
Lawd, say jailer dog you 'roun'.

Says if I had my way wid jailer,
I'd take an' lock him in cell.

I'd take key an' tie it on door,
An' go long way from here, Lawd, Lawd.

Says jail keeper tol' me, Lawd,
Gonna help me get back home.

When time come to be tried,
Jail keeper lied on me.

I told my mother not to worry at all,
Lawd, not to worry at all.

Lawd, goin' to road, mama,
Tryin' to make good time.

Mama, she cried all night long,
O mama, she cried all night long.

Well, she wiped her tears off,
Say, son, she won't cry no more.

Mama come to the road, Lawd,
See her son on the gang.

I tol' her not to bother,
Lawd, cause I got short time.

Once on the gang or in the jail continuous song is not unusual. Waking folk with song in early morning, chanting after meal time, plaintive in the evening, the Negro lives over his past life, gives expression to his feelings, and plans the new day, "standin' on rock pile with ball an' chain," or "standin' on rock pile, with hammer in my hand." He sings of past days, sorrows that some other man will get his girl, boasts a woman in the white man's yard—

My gal she bring me chicken,
My gal she bring me ham,
My gal she bring me everything,
An' she don't give a damn.

Sometimes he is more cheerful and sings, "cawn pone, fat meat, all I gits to eat, better'n I git at home," "Rings on my arms, bracelets on my feet, stronger'n I has at home!" And with bunk for a bed and straw for his head, he sings, "baby, baby, let me be." How could he help falling into the hands of the officers anyway?

'Tain't as Bad as I Said

Good God a'-mighty!
What's a fellow gonna do,
When ol' black mariah [1]
Come a-sailin' after you?

Good God a'-mighty!
My feet's got wings,
Dey can take dis ol' body
Lak she on 'iled springs.

Good God a'-mighty!
She's right 'roun' de corner,
Sho's you bohn,
Dis nigger's a goner.

Good God a'-mighty!
'T ain't bad as I said,
Three square meals a day
An' bunk fer a bed.

The songs that follow will illustrate further the Negro's story of his prison life, his desire for freedom, his efforts to escape, his attitude toward the policeman, jailer and sheriff, and his humorous interpretation of various situations in which he finds himself. Vivid pictures they are.

If I Can Git to Georgia Line

If I can git to Georgia line,
If I can git to Georgia line,
Lawd, if I can git to Georgia line,
Georgia, murderer's home.

Monday I was 'rested,
Tuesday I was fined,
Wednesday I laid in jail,
Thursday I was tried.

---

[1] "Black Mariah" is frequently encountered in Negro songs. It refers to the patrol wagon.

If I can git to Georgia line,
Lawd, if I can git to Georgia line,
O Lawd, if I can git to Georgia line,
Georgia, murderer's home.

Don't ask about it,
If you do I cry.
Don't ask about it,
If you do I cry.

What did redbird, redbird
Say to crow, crow?
You bring rain, rain,
I bring snow, snow!

Friday wid chain gang band,
Saturday pick an' shovel,
Sunday I took my rest,
Monday want to do my best.

Every, every mail day,
Mail day, I gits a letter,
Cryin', "Son, come home,
Lawd, Lawd, come home."

I didn't have no,
No ready money,
I couldn't go home.
No, no, couldn't go home.

I'm on road here
Just a few days longer,
Then I'm goin' home
Law', Law', I'm goin' home.

GOT ME IN THE CALABOOSE

Got me in the calaboose,
Got me in the calaboose,
Got me in the calaboose,
Ain't nobody turn me loose.

Hit's bad, bad on the inside lookin' out,
Hit's bad, bad on the inside lookin' out,

Hit's bad, bad on the inside lookin' out,
This po' boy know what he's talkin' about.

My gal come to the bar and done peep in,
My gal come to the bar and done peep in,
My gal come to the bar and done peep in,
She say, "Honey man, where you been?"

When I git out I ain't gonna stay here,
When I git out I ain't gonna stay here,
When I git out I ain't gonna stay here,
Ain't let nobody treat me dis way.

Po' boy, don't give me no show,
Po' boy, don't give me no show,
Po' boy, don't give me no show,
Ain't gonna be bossed around no mo'.

I Don't Mind Bein' in Jail

I never turn back no more,
Lawd, I never turn back no more,
Every mail day I gets letter from my mother,
Say, "Son, son, come home."

I been fallin' ever since Mary was a baby,
An' now she's gone.
I'm nine hundred miles from home
An' I can't go home this way.

I wish I was a contractor's son,
I'd stand on the bank and have the work well done.
If he don't work, I'll have him hung,
Lawd, if he don't work, I'll have him hung.

I wish I had a bank of my own,
I'd give all the po' workin' men a good happy home.
She used to be mine, look who's got her now.
Sho' can keep her, she don't mean no good to me no mo'.

I laid in jail, back turned to the wall,
Told the jailer to put new man in my stall.
I don't mind bein' in jail
If I didn't have to stay so long. [1]

---

[1] This stanza is found in somewhat different form in the popular song entitled *Jail-House Blues.*

Chain Gang Blues [1]

Standin' on the road side,
Waitin' for the ball an' chain.
Say, if I was not all shackled down
I'd ketch that wes' boun' train.

Standin' on the rock pile
Wid a hammer in my hand,
Lawd, standin' on rock pile,
Got to serve my cap'n down in no-man's land.

The judge he give me sentence
'Cause I wouldn' go to work.
From sunrise to sunset
I have no other clean shirt.

All I got is lovin',
Lovin' an' a-sluggin',
Say I feels just like a stepchild,
Just gi'me the chain gang blues.

Oh, my captain call me
An' my gal work in white folks' yard.
I believe I'll go there too,
'Cause I got the chain gang blues.

My gal she bring me chicken,
My gal she bring me ham,
My gal she bring me everything,
An' she don't give a damn.

My gal she got a molar
Right down below her nose,
She got teeth in her mouth
I'd swear to God was gold.

My gal she cried las' night,
She cried the whole night long;
She cried because judge sentence me,
'Cause I had to go so long.

---

[1] The first four stanzas of this song, except for some slight variations, are also found in *Chain Gang Blues*, a popular phonograph piece.

My gal she cried all night,
I told her not to worry at all.
I'm goin' on the chain gang,
I 'spec' I'll be back in the fall.

All Boun' in Prison [1]

Hey, jailer, tell me what have I done.
Got me all boun' in prison,
Tryin' to 'bide dis woman's time,
Tryin' to 'bide dis woman's time.

Chorus:

All boun' in prison,
All boun' in jail,
Col' iron bars all 'roun' me,
No one to go my bail.

I got a mother and father
Livin' in a cottage by de sea.
I got a sister and a brother, too,
Wonder do dey think o' po' me.

I walked in my room de udder night,
My man walked in and began to fight.
I took my gun in my right han',
Told de folks I'm gonna kill my man.

When I said dat, he broke a stick 'cross my head.
First shot I made my man fell dead.
De paper comed out and strowed de news,
Das why I say I's got de cell-bound blues.

I Went to de Jail House

O Lawd, Lawd, good Lawd, Lawd,
I went to de jail house, fell down on my knees.

I ask that jailer, "Captain, give me back my gal."
Jailer told me, "Sorry, brother, she said her las' good-
bye."

Lawd, I went to judge to ask for a fine.
Judge say, Lawd, he ain't got no time.

---

[1] Cf. phonograph record, *Cell Bound Blues.*

Lawd, I laid in jail so long,
Ain't got no home at all.

Good lawd, look-a here, jail keeper,
Won't you put another gal in my stall?

Say, I been here so long,
Don't know what I'll do.

Judge Gonna Sentence Us So Long

Say, brother, we better get ready to leave jail,
'Cause judge gonna sentence us so long.

Judge gonna sentence us so long,
We ain't gonna come back here no mo'.

Lawd, we have laid in jail so long,
Lawd, we have laid in jail so long.

Say, judge sentence me so long,
He ain't had no mercy on us.

Lawd, captain, come an' got me,
Taken me to road to work.

Lawd, taken me out one mornin',
Taken me out so soon.

Told captain didn't know how to work.
Told me, "Shine, get down that line."

I told the court, Lawd, "Rather be layin' in jail
Wid my back turned to de wall."

I am worried, pretty mama,
But I won't be worried long.

Thought I rather be in my grave
Than be treated like a slave.

Say, rather be in Birmingham
Eatin' pound cake and all.

Say, these women in Georgia
Keep you in trouble all the time.

Say, you better catch your train,
Go to Alabama bound.

I am leavin' here, rider,
Sho' don't want to go.

But I 'spect I have to leave here,
Or I'll be in chain gang, too.

Gonna git me a black woman,
Play safe all the time.

For your brown skin woman
Keep you in trouble all the time.

My Man He Got in Trouble

Mr. T. Bluker,
Don't work my man so hard,
'Cause he's po' player,
Ain't never had no job.

Oh, my man he got in trouble,
He didn't have no friend at all.
They carried him to jail house,
Locked him up in cell.

I asked the judge be light on him.
Judge told him not bring nothin' like that,
Judge give him six months in jail,
Lawd, judge give him six months in jail.

Captain put him on the road.
"Captain, how long have I got?"
Captain say to the shine,
"Eat your supper and run on down the line."

Captain say, "Git your supper,
Lawd, and change your clothes."
Captain say, "Git your supper,
Git your chains and balls."

The Judge He Sentence Me

I laid in the jail with my back to the wall,
I laid in the jail with my back to the wall,
Prayed to the Lord that
Big rock jail would fall.

The judge he sentence me, Lawd,
Give me twelve long months.
The judge he sentence me, Lawd,
Give me twelve long months.

Den captain come take me to de road.
I ask the captain what I gonna do.
Captain told me to pick and shovel too.
I rather be dead, Lawd, and in my grave.

Captain told me,
Say, "Lawd, you ain't gonna work,
Lawd, you ain't gonna work nowhere else
But on this chain gang."

Say, "If I let you go home this time,
You be right back in jail.
When judge gets you again
Gonna give you five long years."

Say, "If you don't quit drinkin'
An' don't quit killin', robbin' and stealin',
You gonna git life time
An' in chain gang, too."

Told captain, "I ain't robbin' no trains,
I swear to God I ain't kill no man."
Lawd, I told the captain, "I ain't robbin' no trains,
Swear to God I ain't kill no man."

I Got a Letter, Captain

I got a letter, captain,
Say, Lawd, come home,
Lawd, captain, come home,
Lawd, say, son, come home.

I don't have, I don't have,
Lawdy, I don't have,
Lawdy, no ready-made money,
An' I can't go home.

I got a gal, Lawd,
Stays right in town.
I got a gal, Lawd,
Stays right in town.

Lawd, street car run
Right by her door,
Lawd, she don't have to walk
Nowhere she go.

Say she take a walk up town,
Lawd, she take a walk up town.
Well, she got in town, Lawd,
An' come back home.

Well, she caught street car
An' come back home.
Lawd, she got street car,
Lawd, Lawd, an' come back home.

PRISONER'S SONG [1]

Wished I had some one to love me,
Some one to call me their own,
Because I'm tired of livin' alone,
Lawd, I'm tired of livin' alone.

I has a gran' ship on de ocean,
Filled wid silver an' gold;
An' befo' my darlin' should suffer,
Dat ship will be anchored an' go.

I'll be carried to de jail tomorrow,
Leavin' my po' darlin' alone,
With the cold prison bars all around me
An' my head on a pillow of stone.

---

[1] Except for a few minor variations, this is the now popular *Prisoner's Song*. It was of folk origin, however.

If I had wings lak an angel,
Over dese prison bars I would fly.
An' I would fly to the arms of my po' darling,
An' dere I'd lay down and die.

Woke up Wid My Back to the Wall

O Lawd, I woke up in the morning,
Woke up wid my back to the wall.
O Lawd, I woke up in the morning,
Woke up wid my back to the wall.

I took a peep out at the bars
O Lawd, I thought I was home.

Lawd, I heard a key rattlin',
High-sheriff comin' in.

Thought I heard a sheriff comin',
Lawd, bring my breakfas' to me.

Thought I see my coffin,
Lawd, rollin' up to my do'.

Lawd, he say, "Dat gal say she don't want you no mo'."
Lawd, I lay right down, hung my head and cried.

Lawd, he say, "Dat gal say she don't want you no mo'."
Lawd, I laid right down in jail and cried.

Lawd, I'm so awful worried till I don't know what to do.
Well, I mistreated Daddy, he hangs 'roun' me day and
  night.

He wakes me in the mornings,
He moans when I am sleepin'.

He makes me swear, Lawd,
Have no other man but you.

In the Negro's prison songs is revealed again that dual nature which sings of sorrowful limitations alongside humorous and philosophical resignation. Here are scenes of the lonesome road illuminated by entertainment of rare quality. "I'm in jail now," he sings, "but jes' fer a day." "I ain't got no parole, but I'm a-comin' back." It is true that he has only corn bread and fat meat to eat but that's "better 'n I has at home." And then with genuine humor he sings also of the iron cuffs about his hands which also are "stronger 'n I has at home."

Better'n I Has at Home

Cawn pone, fat meat,
All I gits to eat—
Better 'n I has at home,
Better 'n I has at home.

Cotton socks, striped clothes,
No Sunday glad rags at all—
Better 'n I gits at home,
Better 'n I gits at home.

Rings on my arms,
Bracelets on my feet—
Stronger 'n I has at home,
Stronger 'n I has at home.

Bunk fer a bed,
Straw under my head—
Better 'n I gits at home,
Better 'n I gits at home.

Baby, baby, lemme be,
Chain gang good enough fer me—
Better 'n I gits at home,
Better 'n I gits at home.

I'm Comin' Back

I write you a letter
Sayin', "Come back home."
I sent you a message,
"Honey, don't you roam."
Comin' back, comin' back,
Hound on my track, yes baby,
I'm comin' back.

Went to de gov'nor,
Ast a parole.
Dat man he answered,
"Not to save yer soul."
Comin' back, comin' back;
Ain't got no parole,
But I'm comin' back.

Lawd, Lawd, I'm comin' back,
Hounds on my track,
Ol' clothes on my back,
Ol' woman in my shack.
No parole, but
I'm comin' back.

GOIN' BACK TO DE GANG

De night wus dark, de guard wus gone,
I slipped dat chain off'n my laig,
De night wus dark, an' de rain hit poured.
Dis nigger astray wid nowhere to board.
I's hungry and cold, nowhere to go,
When de niggers see dese clothes, dey shets de do'.

Out all night, de dawgs am comin',
Goin' back to de gang, tired o' bummin'.
Shin up a tree, no time to be los',
'Cause here's de dawgs, and, golly, de boss!

DEM CHAIN GANG HOUN'S

I ain't no possum, I ain't no squir'l,
But I can shin de highes' tree in all de worl',
When I hear dem houn's, dem chain gang houn's.
Hear dem ol' houn's, soun' goes up to heav'n,
If dey's one dawg, dey mus' be 'lev'n.

Oh, dem houn's, dat ol' lead houn'.
'Tain't good fer a nigger's health to stay on de ground.
Hear dem houn's, dem chain gang houn's.
Come git me, boss, come take me down,
Anything's better 'n de chain gang houn'.

SHOOT, GOOD GOD, SHOOT!

De jedge and de jury
Thought 'twas a shame.
Dey called me up dere,
Axed me my name.

My God a-mighty,
What's a feller gwiner do,
When a nigger gits his wife
An' my wife, too?
Shoot, good God, shoot!

OL' BLACK MARIAH

Look over de hill, see what's a-comin',
Ol' black mariah, natchel-bo'n hummin'.
Drive up to de do', grab me by de collar,
Good Lawd, man, ain't got time to holler.

JES' FER A DAY

I'm 'hind de bars, but jes' fer a day,
'Cause walkin' out de do' ain't de only way.
I've got a saw, and I work like de devil,
All t'ings in dis case am sho' on de level.

ALL US NIGGERS 'HIND DE BARS

I got a gal, you got a gal,
All us niggers got a gal.

He fool 'roun', I fool 'roun',
All us niggers fool 'roun'.

I got a razor, he got a razor,
All us niggers got a razor.

I 'hind de bars, he 'hind de bars,
All us niggers 'hind de bars.

CHAPTER VI

SONGS OF CONSTRUCTION
CAMPS AND GANGS

In the old days—and sometimes in more recent years—there were characteristic and unforgettable scenes of groups of Negroes singing in the fields. Here was a picture of late afternoon in the cotton field, the friendly setting sun a challenge to reviving energies; rows of cotton clean picked, rivalry and cheerful banter, faster picking to the row's end, sacks and baskets full for weighing time; group singing, now joyous, then the melancholy tinge of eventide, *Swing Low, Sweet Chariot, Since I Laid My Burden Down* or *Keep Inchin' Erlong*. Another picture is vivid: A spring morning, a few Negroes following mule and plow, many chopping cotton to the accompaniment of song, all making rhythm of song, movement, and clink of hoe resound in rare harmony, duly interspersed with shouts and laughter. Or the morning yodel or "cornfield holler," with its penetrating vibrato, *Ya-a-ee-ah—oo-a-ee-ou*—indescribable either in words, sound, or musical notation. [1] Or wagons lumbering on cold mornings, drivers and workers on the way to field or mill, songs echoing across the hills. And there were the other group scenes: the roustabouts on the levee, the singers around the cabins, the groups in the kitchen. Many of these scenes, of course, in modified form may yet be found and songs of their setting are still to be heard, but they do not constitute the most commonly abounding characteristic workaday songs of the present.

[1] The phono-photographic record of such a yodel is given in Chapter XV.

Modern scenes, however different, are no less impressive. Whoever has seen a railroad section gang of five score Negroes working with pick and shovel and hammer and bars and other tools, and has heard them singing together will scarcely question the effectiveness of the scene. Likewise steel drivers and pick-and-shovel men sing down a road that is anything but "lonesome" now. Four pickmen of the road sing, swinging pick up, whirling it now round and round and now down again, movement well punctuated with nasal grunt and swelling song. Another group unloading coal, another asphalt, another lime, or sand, sing unnumbered songs and improvisations. Another group sings as workers rush wheelbarrows loaded with stone or sand or dirt or concrete, or still again line up on the roadside with picks and shovels. And of course there are the songs of the chain gangs already described, but nevertheless gang songs of the first importance. All these singers constitute the great body of workers and singers who sing apparently with unlimited repertoire. The selections in this chapter, as in the others, are representative in that they were taken directly from Negro singers and workers in the South during 1924 and 1925.

Among the most attractive of all the Negro workaday songs are those sometimes called "free labor gang songs," [1] of which there are many. Some of these are reserved for Chapter VII in which many miscellaneous examples of songs to help with work are given. Other samples have been included in the "Songs of the Lonesome Road." Examples of the melodies are given in Chapter XV. It will be understood, of course, that other songs such as *John Henry,*

---

[1] The Negroes use the term "free labor" to distinguish ordinary work from convict labor.

Jerry on the Mountain, Lazarus, are sung in this capacity, although classified primarily in other groups for the sake of better illustration.

"FREE LABOR" GANG SONG

Cap'n, did you hear 'bout
All yo' men gonna leave you,
Nex' pay day,
Lawd, Lawd, nex' pay day?

Ev'y mail day,
Mail day, I gits letter,
From my dear ol' mother,
She tell me, "Son, come home."

That ol' letter,
Read about dyin'.
Boy did you ever
Think about dyin'?

Then I can't read it
Now for cryin',
Tears run down,
Lawd, Lawd, tears run down.

Jes' wait till
I make these few days I started,
I'm goin' home,
Lawd, Lawd, I'm goin' home.

Everywhere I
Look this morning,
Look lak rain,
Lawd, Lawd, look lak rain.

I got rainbow
Tied all 'roun' my shoulder,
Ain't gonna rain,
Lawd, Lawd, ain't gonna rain.

Mike an' Jerry
Come down main line Southern,

Didn't stop to get
No water neither coal.

I done walk till
Feets gone to rollin'
Jes' lak a wheel,
Lawd, Lawd, jes' lak wheel.

Now ev'y time I,
Time I start 'round mountain,
My light goes out,
Lawd, Lawd, my light goes out.

I'm gonna buy me
Magnified lantern,
It won't go out,
Lawd, Lawd, it won't go out.

I got a wife,
Two-three children in mountain,
Cryin' fer bread,
Lawd, Lawd, cryin' fer bread.

O LAWD, MAMIE

O Lawd, Mamie,
Poke yo' head out window,
Jes' to see me fall,
Lawd, jes' to see me fall.

I been fallin'
From my shoulder,
Lawd, I been fallin'
All day long.

O Lawd, Mamie,
If I make it
You shall have it,
If it's all in gold.

I been fallin'
Ev'y since Mamie wus baby,
Now she's grown,
Lawd, now she's grown.

When we meet my
Little curly headed woman,
Bow yo' head,
O Lawd, an' tip yo' hat.

If I make it
Through July an' August,
O Lawd, I'll be a man,
O Lawd, I'll be a man.

He-i-Heira

He-he-heira!
Look how my captain stan',
Stand more like a farmer
Than he do a railroad man!

Oh, oh, oh!
If I had listen to what mama said.
I'd be at home now,
Lawd, in mama's bed.

He-i-heira!
Believe I will
Take my pick,
Lawd, over on the hill.

Goin' up town,
Hurry right back,
Gonna see Corinne
When she ball that jack.

Oh, oh, Lawd, oh,
Goin' on up town,
Buy my gal a hat,
Lawd, buy my gal a hat.

She brought it back, Lawd,
Laid it on the shelf
Every time she turn around
Makes her wanter jazz.

Goin' up town, Lawd,
Gonna walk in the yard;

Two-and-a-half hours to work,
Work ain't hard.

O you, down, boys,
Yes, we goin' down.
O you, down, boys,
Yes, we goin' down.

I don't know,
But believe I will
Make my home
In Jacksonville.

Section Boss

Yonder come the engine
Ringin o' the bell;
Engineer on the right,
Fireman on the left.

See the engine makin' time,
See the engineer gone.
Fall off the car,
Throw off the tools.

Throw off the tools,
Let the engine go by.
If I could run like he runs,
I'd run an' never stop.

See the train makin' up speed,
See the cars go 'long.
If I had wings like that engine,
I could run an' fly.

I could pull the bell,
I could blow the whistle,
I could pull the bell,
An' let the engine run.

If I could run like he runs,
I never would quit,
I'd always railroad
I'd always run an' fly.

The mind of the worker and wanderer is perhaps reflected better in his annals of the day's work as expressed in his "captain" songs than anywhere else. Some of the "captain" songs have been sung until they are on the verge of folk songs; some approach the haven of the blues, and many more are in the formative stage. The examples immediately following in this chapter are combinations of all three, with the predominating mode that of combination and improvisation. Some of them are clearly songs of the chain gang as well as of free labor construction work. That they are fairly accurate portrayals of the worker and his task, of the captain and his ways, of the thoughts and customs of the worker and singer will be evident to any one who knows the field. To the uninitiated the laborer is merely a laborer, silent, reserved, certainly keeping back from the white man his innermost thoughts, wishes, and feelings. But hear him sing—hear him repeat the formal songs, hear him make new ones.

O Captain, Captain [1]

O captain, captain,
Where you been so long?
O captain, I been at home
An' done got in trouble again.

O captain, captain,
Won't you be kind?
Don't work me so hard,
Captain, I been used to light work.

O captain, captain,
I ain't used to no hard work.
O captain, captain,
Won't you be light on me?

[1] This song and some others in this chapter are excellent illustrations of the chain gang sentiment becoming mixed with ordinary "free labor" gang songs.

O captain, captain,
If you be light on me,
When I git back home
I won't be hard on you.

O captain, captain,
Where we gonna work?
"Oh, we goin' down the road,
Pick and shovel dirt."

O captain, captain, call me
An' I didn' hear;
Captain took me back
To bodyguard.

O Lawd, captain, captain,
On the side of the bank,
Lawd, Lawd, buddy,
I'm too tired to work.

O captain, captain,
I done got too hot
Captain, O Lawd, captain,
Let po' Shine rest.

Captain, O Lawd, captain,
I set down on a bank,
O Lawd, captain, captain,
Set down on a bank.

O captain, captain,
I cannot work no longer,
'Cause I's done, O Lawd,
Lawd, Lawd, I's done.

O captain, captain,
Po' boy done got too hot,
O Lawd, captain, captain,
An' I couldn't make it go.

Captain, captain,
You got letter from my mother,
Captain, captain,
Read it all the way through.

Lawd, she say, "Son,
Lawd, come back home."
Lawd, Lawd, she say,
"Son, come back home."

Captain, captain,
Ain't got no ready money.
Captain, O Lawd, captain,
Won't you loan me some?

Sittin' in dining room,
O Lawd, captain,
Sittin' in dining room
In yo' chair.

O Lawd, captain,
I aint too dumb,
Hear yo' back door slam,
Lawd God a-mighty.

I got a letter,
Letter from my brown.
My brown she dyin',
Lawd, Lawd, Lawd.

I got a letter,
Letter from my rider.
My rider was dyin',
Lawd, Lawd, Lawd.

Lawd, gonna follow
My brown, Lawd, Lawd.
Gonna follow my brown
To buryin' groun'.

I'm Goin' Back Home

I can jerry, [1] I can jerry
All around the mountain.
Lord, I can jerry, I can jerry
All the way home.

---

[1] The meaning of this expression is uncertain. In other songs it appears as "Hikin' Jerry" or "Mike and Jerry." There is a tradition among the Negro workers that two large mules, named Mike and Jerry, broke loose from their driver and hiked a remarkable distance in one day. If this was the origin of the song, then "I can Jerry" is a result of misunderstanding.

Lord, I see my gal a-comin',
Lord, to bring me my dinner.
Lord, I see my gal a-comin',
Lord, I'm goin' home.

Lord, she brought me something,
Lord, she brought me something good.
Lord, she brought me good dinner,
Didn't know what it was.

Lord, I'm gonna buy me rubber-tire hack,
Lord, I'm gonna buy me rubber-tire hack,
Lord, I'm gonna buy me rubber-tire hack,
Goin' home, take me right back.

I'm tired workin', Lord,
Lord, I'm tired workin'.
Goin' buy me rubber-tire hack,
Take me back home.

Lord, captain standin',
He may hear me sing,
Lord, some old day
I'm goin' back home.

Lord, I reckon I'll sell my,
Lord, I reckon I'll sell my rubber-tire hack
An' buy me a Ford, Lord,
Buy me a Ford.

Lord, captain told me,
O Lord, captain told me,
Time to go to dinner,
Lord, we're goin' back home.

Lord, I got back home
An' had my dinner.
Lord, I went and et,
Lord, I got back home.

Then 'bout half pas' one
Captain call us ail,
Say we got a-go back,
Lord, say we got a-go back to work.

Lord, some o' these mornings,
Lord, some o' these mornings,
Captain ain't gonna hear me sing
'Cause I'm goin' back home.

Sunshine in my back door,
Lord, sunshine in my back door,
Some o' these mornings, Lord, captain,
I'm goin' back home.

Lord, my gal cryin' all day,
Lord, my gal cryin' all day.
Lord, she made a pallet on floor
'Cause she's feelin' right bad.

Captain say, "O Shine,
When you go home,
Say, Shine, you comin' back?"
Yes, captain, O Lord, captain.

Yonder come my girl,
Comin' down the track.
Bring me good cool water,
Keep cool all day long.

I got sun low 'cross the field,
I got sun low 'cross the field plowin'.
Lord, Lord, he tol' me,
O Lord, it was too hot.

Lord, took out the mules,
Lord, I took out my mules
An' went straight home,
'Cause it was too hot.

My Home Ain't Here, Captain

H-e-y- L-a-w-d, Lawd, Lawd,
O Lawd, Lawd, captain

My home ain't here, captain,
An' I ain't got to stay.

I'm goin' back home, captain,
I'm long time sinner, goin' back home.

Ol' Aunty Dinah had candy wagon,
I ast her could I be her driver.

Lawd, Lawd, tol' me "No,"
Lawdy, Lawd, tol' me "No."

O captain, captain, what's matter now?
Ain't thing matter, but I ain't gwine.

Woke up dis mornin' 'bout half pas' fo',
Cap'n call me, but I jes' ain't gonna go.

O Lawd, captain, captain,
How long you gonna hold dis job?

Lawd, captain you look jes' lak new man
Comin', Lawd, on dis job.

Cap'n, captain, will you send me some water,
Ain't had none since dis long mornin'.

All I hate 'bout captain, Lawd,
He want to take me by de tent.

Captain, captain, do you drink co'n liquor?
"Yes, by God, but I ain't got none now."

Captain, captain, when you go to town,
Bring me back a God-damn dram.

Captain, captain, I won't let on,
Lawdy, O Lawdy, captain, I won't let on.

O Lawd, captain, captain, O Lawd,
Won't you let me go home?

Captain tol' me I have to wait,
O Lawd, till I work out my time.

Captain call me an' I laugh,
Cap'n get shoe shine off my britches.

O captain, don't think hard of me,
O Lawd, captain, I don't mean no harm.

Captain, captain, don't mean no harm,
Jes' won't carry on no fun.

Captain, what kin' o' state you come from?
Come from country or come from town?

Captain say, "I come out o' town,
Lawdy, I'll lay yo' body down."

Captain, captain, you look mo' lak farmer
Than you look lak guard man.

CAPTAIN, I'LL BE GONE

O Lawd, captain, hurry, hurry?
Captain, you can't take my time.
What's the use o' hurryin'?
'Cause I got a life time.

Captain, captain, what time o' day?
Captain, captain, what time o' day?
Say he look at Waterbury,
Throw his watch away.

Lawd, captain, captain, did you hear,
Lawd, captain, did you hear about it?
All your men gonna leave you,
All your men gonna leave you on next pay day.

On next pay day, Lawd,
On next pay day, Lawd.
Captain, all your men gonna be gone
On next pay day.

Captain gonna call me some of these mornings,
Lawd, I'm gonna be gone.
Captain gonna call me, go back home,
Lawd, Lawd, I'll be gone.

Wake up one mornin about half pas' fo',
Ask captain could I git drink of water.
Wake up one mornin' about half pas' fo',
Ask captain could I git drink of water.

Captain tol' me to git my pick and shovel,
Git on down the line.
Captain tol' me to git my pick and shovel,
Git on down the line.

Lawd, captain carried me to the road,
Tol' me I had to work.
Tol' my captain I couldn't pick and shovel,
Captain told me have to carry me back to camp.

I ask the captain how long I got.
Captain told me git my shovel,
Say, "Git on down the line,
Lawd, git on down the line."

Say I went to road, captain.
Captain put chains all 'round my legs.
I tol' captain no use to chain me,
'Cause ain't gonna run no mo'.

Captain say, "Yes, I know you won't run,
'Cause I gonna chain you good."
Lawd, say, "Yes, I know you won't run,
'Cause I gonna chain you good."

Captain, captain, little too hard on me,
Lawd, captain little too hard on me.
Captain, captain, I'll be glad to git home;
I'll never come this way no mo'.

Captain called water boy,
Water boy begun to laugh.
Cap'n got shoe shine
Off water boy's pants.

Captain mus' be big,
Weighs two-fifty pounds.
Captain, Lawd, mus' be big,
Weighs two-fifty pounds.

Captain, captain, good long ways,
Lawd, captain, come from Chicago.
I ask the captain the time of day,
Say, "None of you damn business to know."

If I'd A-Known My Cap'n Was Blin' [1]

If I'd a-known my cap'n was blin', darlin',
If I'd a-known my cap'n was blin', darlin',
If I'd a-known my cap'n was blin'
I wouldn' a-went to work till ha'f pas' nine, darlin'.

---

[1] For music see Chapter XIV.

Cap'n, cap'n, you must be cross, darlin',
Cap'n, cap'n, you must be cross, darlin',
Cap'n, cap'n, you must be cross,
Five-thirty an' you won't knock off, darlin'.

When I'm late an' behin', darlin',
When I'm late an' behin', darlin',
When I'm late an' behin',
I can't go to work till ha'f pas' nine, darlin'.

Why I love my cap'n so, darlin',
Why I love my cap'n so, darlin'
Why I love my cap'n so,
Ask him for a dollar an' he give me fo', darlin'.

I Tol' My Cap'n That My Feet Was Col'[1]

I tol' my cap'n that my feet was col'.
"God damn yo' feet, let the car wheel roll."

Cap'n, cap'n, old Ben won't pull.
"God damn his soul, put the harness on the bull."

Cap'n Morgan and Bill Dolin come to line this track,
Pick it up and shake it back.

Cap'n, cap'n the track is wet.
'Knock 'er right on, black boy, till the evenin' sun do set."

Cap'n, cap'n, can you tell
The track is slick and cold as hell?

Captain, Captain, Let Wheelers Roll

Captain, captain, let wheelers roll,
Captain, captain, Lawd, let wheelers roll.

Told my captain hands an' feet wus cold,
Say, "You ought-a warm 'em befo' you come here."

Captain call me early in mo'nin',
Call me to shake six-hoss plow.

I told my captain, captain,
I could not shake dis plow.

---

[1] For music see Chapter XIV.

O captain, captain, what time you gonna quit?
"'Tain't none o' yo' business when I quit."

Gonna buy me ticket, long as my long right arm,
Gonna catch dat train call Cannon Ball.

Goin' to Atlanta, gonna spend de night,
Gonna catch dat train dey call Western Sight.

Goin' to New York an' I aint comin' back,
Lawd, I ain't gonna come back at all.

Say, I'm in trouble, Lawd, Lawd,
I don't know when I'll be back.

Say, if you want to see me, Lawd,
You'll have to come where I am.

Say, I'm long way off, mama,
I ain't comin' back at all.

Have you ever seen risin' sun,
Seen risin' sun turn over?

Lawd, makes me feel low down,
Lawd, lak I'm on my las' go-'round.

Lawd, I hate to see you go,
Make me feel so low down.

Lawd, Lawd, have you ever seen,
Lawd, wild cat hug a lion?

Say, hug him so hard, Lawd,
Wild cat hug him so hard.

Lawd, captain, I'm workin' on road,
An' I'm in trouble again.

Lawd, you won't come see me,
An' I'm workin' in chains.

Lawd, I'm not comin' home no mo',
O Lawd, I'm not comin' home no mo.

Now I don't want you here no mo',
Yo' hair look lak curry comb.

I got brown woman better 'n you,
Lawd, I don't want you no mo'.

'Way up in the Mountain

'Way up in the mountain
Diggin' coal,
All I hates about diggin' coal,
I can't find my parole.

Peach and honey,
Rock and rye,
You can line track
If you try.

Goin' up Church Street,
Comin' down Main,
Huntin' for a woman
That ain't got no man.

Trottin' Liza,
She come a-trottin'
By one this mornin'
With 'er head rag on.

Blues on my mind,
Blues all 'round my head.
I dream last night
That the man I love was dead.

I went to the graveyard,
Fell down on my knees.
I ask the grave-digger
To give me back my railroad man.

The grave-digger,
He looked me in the eye and said,
"I'm sorry to tell you,
But yo' good man is dead."

Thirty days in jail
With my back turned to the wall.
Please, Mr. Jailer,
Put another man in my stall.

I don't mind stayin' there
But I got to stay so long, so long,
Ever' friend I had
Done shook hands an' gone. [1]

Don't You Give Me No Cornbread

I don't want no cornbread, black molasses,
Supper time, O my Lawd, supper time.
Don't you give me cornbread, black molasses,
Supper time, O my Lawd, my supper time.

Don't let the 'gaiter
Beat you to the pone,
Give you mo' trouble
Than days done gone.

Put 'em up solid
An' they won't come down.
When I gets in Illinois
I won't be bothered with the lowland boys.

John the Baptist, he declare
That none but the righteous
Will be there
In the mornin', oh, when I rise.

I got a woman
On Jennielee Square;
If you would die easy,
Let me ketch you there.

The reason I stay
With captain so long,
Ever' morning he give me
Biscuits to rear back on.

Little Evaline
Sittin' in the shade,
Figurin' on the money
I done made.

---

[1] This stanza and the preceding one are also found in a popular song, *Jail-House Blues*.

Captain got a lugger
Tryin' to play bad,
I'm goin' to take it in the mornin'
If he makes me mad.

JULY'S FOR THE RED-BUG

July's for the red-bug,
August for the fly,
I'm diggin' for the bottom,
Bottom must be dry.

I ask my captain
What was the time of day.
Captain got so mad,
Threw his watch away.

I told my captain,
Captain, my feet was cold.
"Doggone your feet, Lawd,
Let the wheelbar' roll."

I told my captain,
Just to keep down trouble,
I reckon I must obey.
Here come the chain gang boss.

But after all there are no workaday songs superior to
the gang songs, heave-a-horas, steel-driving songs,
short pick-and-shovel songs, and the scores of other
short specimens which accompany special tasks re-
quiring hard work, team unison, or continuous effort.
There is, of course, no attempt here to present even an
approach to exhaustive lists. We have so far found
no intimation of where the number of such songs will
stop. But the examples which follow are adequate
to continue the portraiture of the Negro as he works
and as he sings.

Boys, Put Yo' Hands on It

O boys, put yo' hands on it,
O boys, put yo' hands on it,
When I say go, boys, go!

O boys, put yo' hands on it,
O boys, when I holler set it on time,
Everybody goes around.

Say pick up, boys, pick up high,
Goin' line that track steel,
O boys, pick it up high.

Say, boys, when you get back here,
Pick up that steel,
Say, put your hands on it.

Say, boys, put your hands on it,
Everybody goin' to jump at it.
Set it in the bed, boys.

Say, boys, raise your hand higher,
Says, boys, raise your hand higher,
Everybody goin' to jump at it.

Never Turn Back [1]

No mo', oh, no mo'!
No mo', oh, never no mo'!
My Lord
Be here.

I will never
Turn back,
Never turn back
No mo', no mo'.

If you get there
Befo' I do,
Oh, you can tell 'em
I'm comin' too.

I will never turn back,
Never turn back no mo'.

---

[1] Here a spiritual theme is used as a gang song.

An' I would never turn back,
Never turn back no mo'.

Jesus my all
To heaven is gone,
An' whom may I fix
My hopes upon?

No mo', no mo',
No mo', never, my Lawd,
I would never turn back,
Never turn back no mo'.

No More

N o—m o r e,
N o—m o r e,
N o—m o r e,
O—L o r d.

O—L o r d,
O—L o r d,
O—L o r d,
N o—m o r e.

I'm—t h r o u g h,
I'm—t h r o u g h,
I'm—t h r o u·g h,
O—L o r d.

O—L o r d,
O—L o r d,
O—L o r d,
I'm—t h r o u g h.

I'm—t i r e d,
I'm—t i r e d,
I'm—t i r e d,
O—L o r d.

O—L o r d,
O—L o r d,
O—L o r d,
I'm—t i r e d.

I'm—g o i n',
I'm—g o i n',
I'm—g o i n',
O—L o r d.

O—L o r d,
O—L o r d,
Y e s, O—L o r d,
I'm—t i r e d.

ALL RIGHT

A l l—r i g h t,
O—L o r d,
A l l—r i g h t,
P u s h—o n.

A l l—r i g h t,
O—L o r d,
L e t's—g o,
L i t t l e—m o'.

A l l—r i g h t,
O—L o r d,
G e t—i t—o v e r,
L e t's—g o.

A l l—r i g h t,
O—L o r d,
G e t—a r o u n d—i t—b o y s,
L e t's—g o.

A l l—r i g h t—b o y s,
P i c k—i t—u p,
G a n g—a r o u n d—i t,
L e t's—g o.

HELP ME DRIVE 'EM [1]

O King's Mountain,
O King's Mountain,
O King's Mountain,
    So high!

---

[1] This is an example of a steel-driving song. As the driver raises his hammer he sings a line, then stops singing for a moment, brings the hammer down with a grunt, then sings another line, and so on. The technique is the same as the digging technique described in some detail in Chapter XIV.

O run here, buddy,
O run here, buddy,
O run here, buddy,
    O boy!

O help me drive 'em,
O help me drive 'em,
O help me drive 'em,
        All day!

I BELONG TO STEEL-DRIVIN' CREW

O shake 'em up, buddy,
An' I'll drive 'em down;
O shake 'em up, buddy,
An' I'll drive 'em down;
I belong to steel-drivin' crew,
Lawd, I belong to steel-drivin' crew.

O lovin' buddy,
Where you been so long?
O lovin' buddy,
Where you been so long?
I belong to steel-drivin' crew,
Lawd, I belong to steel-drivin' crew.

O BUCKEYE RABBIT

The rabbit run, the rabbit jumped,
The rabbit skipped the river.
O buckeye rabbit, hey, hey!
O buckeye rabbit, Susan!
O buckeye rabbit, hey, hey!
The rabbit skipped the river!

U—H, U—H, LAWDY [1]

U—h, u—h, Lawdy,
I wonder why
I got to live
Fer de by an' de by.

---

[1] This is an example of a pick song, although it could be used, of course, for almost any kind of rhythmic work. For a description of the singing-digging technique see Chapter XIV.

U—h, u—h, Lawdy,
Don't you bother me.
I'm always mighty happy
When I'm on a spree.

U—h, u—h, Lawdy,
U—h, u—h, Lawdy,
U—h, u—h, Lawdy,
U—h, Lawdy, u—h, Lawdy, po' me!

This Ol' Hammer

This ol' hammer, hammer
Mus' be loaded;
This ol' hammer, hammer
Mus' be loaded;
This ole' hammer, hammer
Mus' be loaded;
Do bear down,
Do bear down.

Bitin' spider, where did
You leave trottin' Sallie?
Bitin' spider, where did
You leave Trottin' Sallie?
Bitin' spider, where did
You leave Trottin' Sallie?
In Birmingham, O Lawd,
In Birmingham.

We Are Clambin' Jacob's Ladder [1]

Get 'em over yonder,
Get 'em long,
Get 'em short.
Lord, get 'em over yonder,
Get 'em over yonder.

We are clambin', clambin'
Jacob's ladder,
Jacob's ladder.
Oh, we are clambin' Jacob's ladder,
Almos' home, yes, almos' home.

[1] Here a theme from a spiritual is made to do service as a pick song.

Every little roun' gets
Higher and higher,
Higher and higher.
Every little roun' gets higher and higher,
Almos' home, home, almos' home.

Reason I Stay on Job So Long [1]

Reason I stay on job so long,
Lawd, dey gimme flamdonies
An' coffee strong.

Reason I love my captain so,
'Cause I ast him for a dollah,
Lawd, he give me fo'.

Reason why I love Boleen,
She keeps my house
An' shanty clean.

Why I like Roberta so,
She rolls her jelly
Like she do her dough.

Hot Flambotia an' Coffee Strong

Reason I stay on job so long,
Oh, reason I stay on job so long,
O Lawd, reason I stay on job so long:
Hot flambotia an' coffee strong.

Hot flambotia an' coffee strong,
Yes, Lawd, hot flambotia an' coffee strong.
O Lawd, hot flambotia an' coffee strong,
Reason I stay on job so long.

I'm Goin' On [2]

I'm gonna row here,
I'm gonna row here,
I'm gonna row here few days longer,
Then, Lawd, I'm goin' on.

---

[1] For music see Chapter XIV.
[2] This song has been heard also as "I'm on road here few days longer" and "I'm gonna roll here few days longer." "Row" may well be a corruption of "road" or "roll."

Oh, I'm gonna row here,
Lawd, I'm gonna row here,
Yes, Lawd, I'm gonna row here few days longer,
Then I'm goin' on.

Yes, Lawd, I'm goin' on,
Then, Lawd, I'm goin' on,
Yes, Lawd, I'm gonna row here few days longer,
Then I'm goin' on.

I Don't Want No Trouble With de Walker [1]

I don't want no,
Want no trouble with de walker.
I don't want no,
Want no trouble with de walker.
I wanta go home,
Lawd, Lawd, I wanta go home.

Oh, me an' my buddy
Jes' came here this mornin'.
Wanta go home,
Lawd, Lawd, wanta go home.

I can drive it,
Drive it long as anybody.
Wanta go home,
Lawd, Lawd, wanta go home.

Cap'n, did you hear about,
Hear about two your womens gonna leave you?
Wanta go home,
Lawd, Lawd, wanta go home.

I'm gonna roll here, [2]
Roll here a few days longer.
I'm goin' home,
Lawd, Lawd, I'm goin' home.

---

[1] This is a pick song commonly heard around Chapel Hill, N. C. The "walker" refers to the walking boss or overseer on the job. The first two lines of each stanza are repeated as shown in the first stanza. For music see Chapter XIV.

[2] See footnote, p. 112.

Cap'n an' walker,
Walker been raisin' san'.
Cap'n told walker
He could git 'im another man.

Lawd, dey got my buddy,
Buddy an' his forty-fo!
Next 'lect'ocution
Dey'll git him sho'.

I DON'T WANT NO CORNBREAD [1]

I don't want no, [2]
Want no cornbread, peas, an' molasses;
I don't want no,
Want no cornbread, peas, an' molasses,
At supper time,
Lawd, Lawd, at supper time.

Oh, hand me down a
Can o' corn an' tomatoes,
For my meal,
Lawd, Lawd, for my meal.

My little woman,
She don't treat me like she used to.
No she don't,
Lawd, Lawd, no she don't.

She used to feed me,
Feed me on biscuits an' butter
For my meal,
Lawd, Lawd, for my meal.

She used to give me,
Give me lots o' huggin' every mornin'.
Now she don't,
Lawd, Lawd, now she don't.

---

[1] This is sung to the same tune as the preceding song, *I Don't Want No Trouble With the Walker*, the music of which is given in Chapter XIV.
[2] All of the stanzas have this form, first two lines always repeated.

Turning from the songs of construction or railroad gangs, some of the mixed songs, partly remnants of former years, partly products of sophistication, may be cited. There are many songs about the white man and the captain, excellent samples of which have already been cited in this chapter. Some were given in *The Negro and His Songs* and many more are to be found. Indeed, songs about the white man may well constitute a separate chapter in a later volume. A stock joke among the older Negroes used to be that of telling how the white man always brought "nigger out behind." The modern singer, albeit not always in joking mood, still thrusts "at" his "captain" or "boss" or "white man." "Captain," he sings, "you look mo' lak farmer than railroad man," and with considerable glee asks, "Captain, captain, where'd you come frum?" On the other hand, reminiscent of farm days and echoing current life, he still sings:

> Niggers plant the cotton,
> Niggers pick it out,
> White man pockets money,
> Niggers does without.

In another song the Negro complained that no matter if he worked all the time, "Boss sho' bring nigger out behin'." So now in some Georgia scenes he sings:

Nothin' to Keep

> Up at fo' 'clock,
> Work till dark,
> Wages han,'
> I'm de man.
> Twelve a month an' boa'd,
> Lawd, twelve a month an' boa'd.
>
> Hope I die,
> Mo' I try,
> I comes out

Owin' boss mo',
I comes out,
Lawd, owin' boss mo'.

Plenty to eat,
Place to sleep,
All night to stray about;
But nothin' fer a feller,
Lawd, nothin' fer
A feller to keep.

EVERYBODY CALL ME THE WAGES MAN

Early in the spring I'm plowin' my lan',
Early in the spring I'm plowin' my lan',
Early in the spring I'm plowin' my lan',
Everybody calls me the wages man,
　　Baby, baby.

Next down de row with guano horn,
Next down de row with guano horn,
Next down de row with guano horn,
Never work so hard since I've been born,
　　Baby, baby.

Little bit later I swings de hoe,
Little bit later I'swings de hoe,
Little bit later I swings de hoe,
I'se de nigger dat leads de row,
　　Baby, baby, baby.

Sack an' basket all that I pick,
Sack an' basket all that I pick,
Sack an' basket all that I pick,
Never stop for nothin', even if you sick,
　　Baby, baby.

White man in starched shirt settin' in shade,
White man in starched shirt settin' in shade,
White man in starched shirt settin' in shade,
Laziest man that God ever made,
　　Baby, baby.

MISSUS IN DE BIG HOUSE

Missus in de big house,
Mammy in de yard.
Missus holdin' her white hands,
Mammy workin' hard,
Mammy workin' hard,
Mammy workin' hard.
Missus holdin' her white hands,
Mammy workin' hard.

Ol' marse ridin' all time,
Niggers workin' 'roun'.
Marse sleepin' day time,
Niggers diggin' in de groun',
Niggers diggin' in de groun',
Niggers diggin' in de groun'.
Marse sleepin' day time,
Niggers diggin' in de groun'.

CHAPTER VII

JUST SONGS TO HELP WITH WORK

IN some respects it is unfortunate that classification of the Negro workaday songs must be attempted, for, strictly speaking, accurate classification is not possible. There is much overlapping apparent in most of the best types. There are mixed pictures in the majority and a cross index would be necessary for any sort of complete analysis. And yet the total picture is clearer when the songs are grouped according to prevailing themes, as has been done in other chapters on the wanderer songs, the bad man ballads, chain gang and jail songs, favorites of the construction gang, songs of woman, songs of man, and religious remnants. In each of these classes it is readily seen that there is abundance of new material of great value. And yet, after these attempts at classification, there are scores of songs, some the favorites of the present day, some among the most attractive, which appear best as simple work songs, sung as an integral physical part of the Negro's workaday efforts. These songs are not simply the "miscellaneous" and "all others" group. They are more than that; they are the songs for song's sake, expression for expression's sake, and "hollerin' jes' to he'p me wid my work."

This chapter, therefore, presents a varied group of songs, many of which, for simple spontaneity, imagery, and creative art might well represent the choice of the collection. Among these are the lyric types like those quoted in Chapter I, figures of a "rainbow 'round my shoulders," the "feet rollin' lak a wheel," the winter song in summer, and many other fragments of similar quality. There are fragments, pick-and-shovel songs, driving songs, mostly short, which are sung perhaps more often than any others by the group of workers. This chapter will present, first, some of the miscellaneous and more artistic songs that are most difficult to classify except as "just songs to help with work." Then will follow certain types, corruptions from blues, jazz and minstrel, but sung on any and all occasions, one as well as another, in the kitchen, on the road, in the field, in the alley, in the barber shop, or on the street. Then, finally, there will be the group of incoherent words and lines, senseless for the most part and merely expressive of feeling and effort. In addition to these there are still more than one hundred miscellaneous songs, improvisations, fragments and other collected items which must await a special collection of this sort.

One of the most attractive of all the work songs is *Mule on the Mountain*, in which the title constitutes the bulk of the song. It is a pick-and-shovel favorite repeated over and over with variations and exclamations. The simplest form of this song is as follows:

MULE ON THE MOUNTAIN

Mule on mountain
Called Jerry,
I can ride 'im
Any time I want to;
Lawd, I can ride 'im
Any time I want to.

In the following version this simple stanza has taken seven others for companions, thus making a lengthy pick song.

I GOT A MULIE [1]

I got a mulie,
Mulie on the mountain, call 'im Jerry.
I got a mulie,
Mulie on the mountain, call 'im Jerry.
I can ride 'im,
Ride 'im any time I want to,
Lawd, Lawd, all day long.

Lawd, this ol' mountain,
Mountain must be hanted,
My light goes out,
Lawd, Lawd, my light goes out.

I'm gonna buy me,
Buy me a magnified lantern.
'Twon't go out,
Lawd, Lawd, won't go out.

I'm gonna buy me,
Buy me a winchester rifle,
Box o' balls,
Lawd, Lawd, box o' balls.

I gonna back my,
Back myself in the mountains
To play bad,
Lawd, Lawd, to play bad.

Mike an' Jerry [2]
Must be a gasoline burner;
Didn't stop here,
Lawd, Lawd, didn't stop here.

Mike an' Jerry
Hiked from Jerome to Decatur [3]
In one day,
Lawd, Lawd, in one day.

---

[1] For music see Chapter XIV.
[2] See footnote, p. 96.
[3] Probably refers to Rome and Decatur, Georgia. The distance between these two places is about a hundred miles, a pretty good "hike" for the mules if they made it in one day!

Didn't stop here, Lawd,
To get no coal, neither water,
Hiked on by,
Lawd, Lawd, hiked on by.

Very much after the same manner and type is the pick-and-shovel song, *Lookin' over in Georgia*, which apparently has nothing specific as its historical base and no more sense to it than *Mule on the Mountain*.   And yet it is one of the prettiest of Negro songs when accompanied by group movement, rhythm, and harmony.

LOOKIN' OVER IN GEORGIA

Well I can stan',
Lookin' 'way over in Georgia;
Well I can stan',
Lookin' 'way over in Georgia;
Well I can stan',
Lookin' 'way over in Georgia,
O-eh-he, Lawd, Lawd,
She's burnin' down,
Lawd, she's burnin' down.

For sheer artistry, however, one would have to search a long time to find a superior to the following verses, sung by a young Negro workingman, on platform and swing, washing the brick walls of a newly constructed university building.

BEAR CAT DOWN IN GEORGIA

I'll be back here,
I'll be back here,
Lawd, Lawd,
I'll be back here.

Bear cat, Lawd,
Bear cat, Lawd,
Turn to lion
Down in Georgia.

Look-a yonder,
Look-a yonder,
Lawd, Lawd,
Down in Georgia.

Ever see bear cat
Turn to lion,
Lawd, Lawd,
Down in Georgia?

My ol' bear cat,
My ol' bear cat
Turn to lion,
Lawd, Lawd, Lawd.

Ever see a bear cat
Hug a lion,
Lawd, Lawd,
Down in Georgia?

If I make it,
If I make it,
Lawd, Lawd,
Down in Georgia.

Lord, I been fallin',
Lord, I been fallin',
Lawd, Lawd,
From my place.

'Fo' long, Lawd,
Yes, 'fo' long, Lawd,
I'll be back here,
I'll be back here.

Scarcely less mixed and informal is the delightful song *Shoot that Buffalo* sung in low undertone suitable to any sort of work such as digging, cutting, laying rock, unloading coal or gravel, or doing domestic duties. The melody of this "song just to help with work" is presented in Chapter XIV.

Shoot That Buffalo

Went down to Raleigh,
Never been there befo',
White folks on the feather-bed,
Niggers on the flo'.

Chorus:

> Shoot that buffa-,
> Shoot that -lo,
> Shoot that buffalo.

Went down to low groun'
To gather up my corn,
Raccoon sot the dogs on me,
'Possum blowed his horn.

Las' year was a bad crop year,
Ev'ybody knowed it.
I didn't make but a bushel o' corn
An' some damn rascal stoled it.

I had ol' back-band,
It was made out o' leather;
Kept me all the doggone time
Keepin' it sewed together.

One of the bad man songs listed in Chapter IV was *Dupree,* of which two versions were presented. The following song was sung by a young Negro recently from the chain gang. It purports to be a song made up by Dupree while in prison. As a matter of fact it is a composite jumble composed largely while being sung. It illustrates well the general situation in which any song of any sort will do just as well as any other.

Dupree's Jail Song

I don't want no coal-black woman for my regular,
Give me brown, Lawd, Lawd, give me brown.

Black woman study evil,
That's why I want brown, yes, yes, give me brown.

I'm gonna roll here a few days longer,
Then I'm goin' home, yes, then I'm goin' home.

Don't you hear those rein-deers cryin'?
But it ain't gonna rain, no, no, ain't gonna rain.

If it rain I can't see Betty,
That's why it ain't gonna rain.

Every mail day I get a letter
Saying, "Daddy, come home, yes, yes, daddy, come
   home."

Some of these days I'll see Betty,
An' it won't be long, no, no, it won't be long.

If I could see her just one mo' time,
My mind would be changed all the time.

The jailer told Dupree, "Just be good,"
And he surely would, yes, yes, he surely would.

Dupree was the best man in the pen
Just to get that thing, yes, yes, that thing.

Another illustration of the common promiscuity of these current songs adapted as a part of the physical effort of work is the following mongrel song of the self-styled bad man who mixes metaphors and lines to his own satisfaction.

I'm Goin' out West

When you see me comin'
Wid my new shine on,
'Cause I got my col'-iron burner [1]
Under my ol' left arm.

Lawd, I goin' out West,
Goin' out 'mongst the robbers.
Say, if I don't get back,
Lawd, don't worry at all.

---

[1] That is, his pistol.

'Cause the Western men call theirself bad,
'Cause the Western men call theirself bad.
Say, when they get unruly,
Say, I got their water on.

Say, my gal lay down,
Lay down and cried
'Cause I's goin' out West,
But I'm satisfied.

Say, I grab an' hug an' kiss her,
Say, don't worry at all,
'Cause I'm goin 'way from here,
Goin' to kill some rowdy men.

I reach down an' kiss my gal,
Kiss an' hug her all day long,
Lawd, she make me so much worry
I had to leave home.

The selections that follow are typical of the large number of miscellaneous songs of almost every imaginable mixture and variety. They are examples of corruptions and also of the song-making process and of the insignificance of words and meaning in the workaday song.

Julia Long

O Lawd, Aunt Julia!
Julia Long, Julia Long!
O Lawd, Aunt Julia!
Julia Long, Julia Long.

Julia Long, dead and gone,
Julia Long, Julia Long!
O Lawd, Aunt Julia!
Julia Long, Julia Long!

Julia Long I used to know,
Julia Long, Julia Long.
O Lawd, Aunt Julia!
Julia Long, Julia Long!

TURN YO' DAMPER DOWN

When you see me comin'
Raise yo' winder high,
When you see me leavin'
Hang yo' head an' cry.

I got lovin'
Way a rabbit hug a houn',
An' if you two-time me, daddy,
Turn yo' damper down.

CASEY JONES [1]

Casey was goin' about ninety-four,
An' he forgot to blow.
Casey told the fireman he'd better jump,
For there's two locomotives that's about to bump.

Chorus:

Casey Jones, marchin' to the cabin,
Marchin' to the cabin with the orders in his hand.

Casey said before he died,
"Three mo' roads I want to ride."
The fireman ask him what could they be,
"Southern Pacific an' the Santa Fe."

Casey told his children,
"Go to bed and hush your cryin',
You have another papa
On the Salt Lake Line."

WASH MY OVERHALLS

Wash my overhalls,
Search my overhalls,
Starch my overhalls,
Wash 'em clean,
'Cause I'm goin' to ketch de train.

---

[1] *Casey Jones* is still heard occasionally. The version given here is somewhat below par, but represents the sort of thing a worker is likely to sing. Note that Casey wants to ride "three mo' roads," but names only two. Also, in the last stanza, Casey, instead of his wife, is represented as speaking to the children.

Listen at dis fireman blow de train.
If I don't ring dat bell,
You ring it fer yo'self;
If you don't ring it,
Won't be no fault o' mine.

Dove Came Down by the Foot of My Bed

Dove came down by the foot of my bed,
By the foot of my bed,
By the foot of my bed,
Dove came down by the foot of my bed,
And he carried the news that I was dead.

I'm going away one day before long,
One day before long,
One day before long.
I'm going away one day before long,
And I won't be back before judgment day.

If you don't believe I've been redeemed,
I've been redeemed,
I've been redeemed.
If you don't believe I've been redeemed,
Just follow me down by Jordan stream.

Dig my grave and dig it deep,
Dig it deep,
Dig it deep.
Dig my grave and dig it deep,
And cover me up with a linen sheet.

Tell my mother if she wants to see me,
If she wants to see me,
If she wants to see me,
Tell my mother if she wants to see me,
She must ride that horse in the battlefield.

He Wus de Gov'nor of Our Clan

He wus de gov'nor of our clan,
He wus a rough-an'-tumble man,
He wus a rough-an'-tumble man.
He pull his pistol an' a feller drap,
He make his money playin' crap,
He make his money playin' crap.

I Got Chickens on My Back

I got chickens on my back,
An' the white folks on my track,
I am hunting for a shanty,
God knows, nobody knows.
I am hunting for a shanty,
God knows, nobody knows.

I Ain't Gonna Let Nobody Make a Fool Out o' Me

I've been all over the U. S. A.,
I've seen most everything;
I've shot craps with the president,
Played cards with the queen and king.
But I ain't gonna let nobody,
Nobody make a fool out o' me.

If you give your gal everything she needs,
You will spend the winter in your B. V. D.'S.
I ain't gonna let nobody,
Nobody make a fool out o' me.

On My Las' Go-'Round [1]

I had it in my head to join the U. S. A.,
But instead of gettin' better I got still worse.
Every time I hear some church bell ringin',
I begin to think I was on my las' go-'round.
O I believe I am on, I think I am on,
I know I am on my las' go-'round.
So when I am dead, wear no black,
When Gable blows his trumpet I'll rush on back.

Berda, You Come too Soon

O Lord, Berda, you come too soon,
Found a man in my saloon.
Berda walked out screamin' an cryin',
Girls on front street skippin' an' flyin'.
Berda, you come too soon,
Berda, you come too soon.

---

[1] There are now popular songs entitled *Last Go-'Round Blues* and *I'm on My Last Go-'Round*, but they do not resemble this song. For an older version, see *The Negro and His Songs*, p. 180.

Rain or Shine

I hoes an' I plows
In all kinds o' weather,
I got to keep a-goin'
'Cause I can't do no better.

Rain or shine,
Sleet or snow,
When I gits done dis time,
Won't work no mo'.

Empty or full,
Sleep or 'wake,
I'm gwine to de party,
Dance fer dat cake.

Who's Goin' to Buy Your Whiskey?

Who's goin' to buy your whiskey
When I'm gone away from you?
Who's goin' to do your holdin'
When I'm gone from you, Lawd, Lawd?
Who's goin' to bring you chicken
From the white folks' house
When I'm gone away from you?

You Calls Me in de Mornin'

You calls me in de mornin',
You calls me in de night,
An' you is de cause o' me
Losin' my life.
My home ain't here, I don't have to stay.
When I leaves don't wear no black,
Do, I sho' gonna come creepin' back,
Do, I sho' gonna come creepin' back.

Dig-a My Grave Wid a Silver Spade

Dig-a my grave wid a silver spade,
Let me down wid a golden chain.
Oh, who's gonna dig-a my grave?
Let me down wid a golden chain.
Yonder come mudder,
Look lak mudder comin' on.
Oh, who's gonna dig-a my grave?

Yonder Come de Devil

Yonder come de devil,
Yonder come de devil,
Ketch him, devil, ketch him,
Ketch him, devil, ketch him.
He done sin, he done sin,
He done sin, he done sin.
Ketch him, devil, ketch him,
Ketch him, devil, ketch him.

Dem Turrible Red Hot Blues [1]

Nothin' new,
Her name wuz Sue,
I got de turrible
Red hot blues,
Oh, dem turrible red hot blues.
I got a pal,
This gal is Sal,
Bofe got de turrible red hot blues,
Oh, dem turrible red hot blues.

Das 'Nough Said

Hit rains, hit hails,
Different sorts o' wedder,
Hit rains, hit hails,
Wusser de better.
Steal up to de back do'
Den on to de bed,
Lawsy, lawsy, mister,
Das 'nough said.

Diamond Joe

Diamond Joe wants a sack of flour,
Diamond Joe wants a sack of flour,
Diamond Joe he don't work by de hour.
Drive on, Diamond Joe.
Sometimes he works in de country,
Sometimes he works in de town,
Sometimes he has a good notion
To jump in de river an' drown.
Drive on, Diamond Joe.

[1] Compare *Red Hot Blues*, a popular phonograph and sheet music piece.

HE RUN ME IN

Talkin' 'bout yo' ghosts, let me tell:
I thought I drapped dat nigger in dat well
But he run me in, yes, Lawd, he run me in.
'Tain't no fun I's here to tell
When a dead nigger gits out'n an ol' fiel' well
An' runs me in, yes, Lawd, he run me in.

He ain't got no arms, he ain't got no haid,
I didn't stop an' count dem tracks I made,
'Cause he run me in, yes, Lawd, he run me in.
I believes in a ghost an' I believes in a hant
Dis here nigger sho' ain't no saint,
'Cause he run me in, yes, Lawd, he run me in.

DE GOAT'S GOT A SMELL

De goat's got a smell,
De skunk's got a stink,
But de black gal
Got a 'culiar odor.
De black gal, de balmoral,
Dey bofe got a 'culiar odor.

GOODBY SOOKIE

Goodby, Sookie, good by, Sal,
You struts about in dat balmoral.
Goodby, Sookie, good by, Sal
I's leavin' dis hot town wid dat yellow gal.

OUT IN DE CABIN

Out in de cabin, banjo pickin' low;
Out in de cabin, banjo pickin' low.
Up in de big house, singin' soft an' low;
Up in de big house dancin' to an' fro.
I lubs my missus, I lubs ol' marse;
I lubs my white folks mo' an' mo',
Mo' an' mo'.

Darlin' Get on de Road

Darlin', when you see me comin',
Hang your head an' cry.
When you see me leavin',
Get on the road.
Darlin', get on the road,
Darlin', get on the road.

When you see me cryin',
Hang you head in shame.
When you see me smilin',
You know I am the same.
So let us get on the road,
Darlin', get on the road.

I'm Gonna Have Me a Red Ball All My Own

Lawd, lissen, I believe I go to town
An' ketch the Red Ball. [1]
An' I walked up to get in.
What you reckin the man said to me?
"No nigger can ride the Red Ball."
So I turned around an' went back home
An' began to paint my face.
But I forgot to paint my neck an' hands.
So I went back an' tried him again.
Didn't have no luck. An' I'm
Gonna get me a mule an' name him Red Ball,
An' I can ride just the same.
I'm gonna have me a Red Ball all my own.

Great Scots, You Don't Know What to Do

Bull frog sittin' on mantel-piece,
Great scots, you don't know what to do,
Clapped his hand in a pan of grease,
Great scots, you don't know what to do.
I'm going down in new town to live.

---

[1] A fast freight train.

Look out, ladies, let him by,
You don't know what to do,
Here he comes with a greasy eye,
Great scots, you don't know what to do.
I'm going down in new town to live.

Chicken Never Roost too High fo' Me [1]

Ol' massa's chicken
Live in the tree,
Chicken never roost
Too high fo' me.

Went out strollin',
See what I can see.
Chicken never roost
Too high fo' me.

Ever since the Yankee
Set-er me free,
Chicken never roost
Too high fo' me.

They think the old lady
An' me agree.
Chicken never roost
Too high fo' me.

I's in jail,
Not long till I'm free,
Chicken never roost
Too high fo' me.

Stewball Was a Racer [2]

Stewball was a racer,
Mollie was too.
My mist'iss bets by hundred,
My master bets by thousands.

[1] In a somewhat different version, this song was popular as a minstrel
some twenty years ago.
[2] This is a fragment of a song, *Skewball*, which used to be almost an epic
among the Negroes. Its origin probably goes back to an old Irish song.
For a discussion of this point, see Scarborough, *On the Trail of Negro Folk-
Songs*, pp. 61-4.

I bet you mo' cash money
Ol' Stewball won.
Run on, ol' Stewball,
Mollie done run.

Shanghai Rooster

Shanghai rooster done lost all his feathers,
Shanghai pullet eat by her betters.
You gits de gizzard, I eats the breast,
Got to save the preacher all the rest.
Chicken wid a preacher don't stand no show,
When the preacher is about chicken gotta go.

Went over to fishin' on a little stream,
All I got is a nod and dream.
Catch Miss Catfish by the snout,
Led Miss Catfish all about.

CHAPTER VIII

MAN'S SONG OF WOMAN

THERE is probably no theme which comes nearer being common to all types of Negro songs than the theme of the relation of man and woman. It is the heart and soul of the blues. The Negro bad man is often pictured as being bad because of a woman. The jail and chain gang songs abound in plaintive references to woman and sweetheart, and the worker in railroad gang and construction camp often sings to his "cap'n" about his woman. Likewise, in the songs of woman, man plays the leading rôle. These man and woman songs are of such significance that special attention must be given to them as a type of Negro song in order to round out the picture of Negro workaday life which this volume is trying to present. In this chapter and the one following, therefore, there have been brought together examples of songs which deal primarily with the relation of the sexes.

Conflicts, disagreements, jealousies and disappointments in the love relation have ever been productive of song. They are the chief source of "hard luck" songs or blues, and the Negro's naïve way of singing of his failure and disappointments in love is what has made the blues famous. Sometimes his songs portray vividly, often with a sort of martyr-like satisfaction, his difficulties with women. At times his song is defiant. At other times it is merely a complaint. Again, it is despondent, in which case he is going "to jump in the rivuh an' drown" or "drink some pizen down" or do something else calculated to make the woman sorry that she mistreated him. Some of the "hard luck" stories of the Negro man are told in the following group of songs.

Lawd, She Keep on Worryin' Me

Lawd, Lawd, she keep on worryin' me,
Lawd, captain, she keep on worryin' me.

Lawd, she cry all night long,
Lawd, Lawd, she cry all night long.

Mama, the mo' I pet her, Lawd,
The mo' I pet her the mo' she cries.

Lawd, I gonna give her mouf full o' fist
An', Lawd, she won't cry no mo'.

Captain, captain, I don't bother nobody,
Works every day as bes' I can.

Captain, look like you could make her,
Lawd, leave me alone.

Captain, she say she love me
Like school boy love his pie.

Lawd, she say I leave her alone,
Lawd, ain't got no friends at all.

My Girl She's Gone and Left Me

My girl, she's gone and left me,
She left me all alone,
She promised that she would marry me
The day that she left home.

So kiss me, all you brown skins
And all you yellows, too.
I would give anything in this wide, wide world
Just because I do love you.

Dat Brown Gal Baby Done Turn Me Down

I's goin' down to de rivah,
Jump in an' drown,
Dat brown gal baby
Done turn me down,
Done turn me down.

Goin' down to de drug sto',
Pisen I drink down,
Den dey take de news
To my baby brown,
To my baby brown.

Call up de doctah
Mighty quick,
Tell my brown baby
I sho' is sick,
I sho' is sick.

Den my black baby
Come hurryin' 'roun',
She sho' be sorry
She turn me down,
She turn me down.

I Brung a Gal From Tennessee

Ain't yer heard my po' story?
Den listen to me:
I brung a gal from Tennessee
Tennessee, Tennessee
I brung a gal from Tennessee.

Ain't yer heard my po' story?
Den listen to me:
Dat Georgia gal set de police on me.
Tennessee, Tennessee,
I brung a gal from Tennessee.

Don't Wanta See Her No Mo'

I ain't never seed her befo',
I ain't never seed her befo',
I ain't never seed her befo',
Don't wanta see her no mo', baby.

She say, "Come on, go to my house,"
She say, "Come on, go to my house,"
She say, "Come on, go to my house,"
She ain't nuffin but a roust-about, baby.

She s'arch my pockets through,
She s'arch my pockets through,
She s'arch my pockets through,
Den say, "I ain't got no need of you, baby."

Don't e'r wanta see her no mo',
Don't e'r wanta see her no mo',
Don't e'r wanta see her no mo',
Never had seed her befo', baby.

I's Havin' a Hell of a Time

I's a-havin' a hell of a time,
I's a-havin' a hell of a time,
I's a-havin' a hell of a time,
Livin' wid dese two women o' mine.

De po' boy, dey got no mercy at tall,
De po' boy, dey got no mercy at tall,
De po' boy, dey got no mercy at tall,
Dey lock in de room, he sets out in de hall.

Ain't gonna stay here no mo',
Ain't gonna stay here no mo',
Ain't gonna stay here no mo',
De creepers all 'roun' my do'.

Goin' back down to Georgia lan',
Goin' back down to Georgia lan',
Goin' back down to Georgia lan',
Where women don't have jes' one man.

Yer don't haf to have no clo'es,
Yer don't haf to have no clo'es,
Yer don't haf to have no clo'es,
De women don't never lock deir do's.

Lawdy, What I Gonna Do?

U—h, Lawdy, what I gonna do?
U—h, Lawdy, what I gonna do?
U—h, Lawdy, what I gonna do?
Been havin' jes' ol' lady, but now I got two, baby!

U—h, Lawdy, ol' lady got rough,
U—h, Lawdy, ol' lady got rough,
U—h, Lawdy, ol' lady got rough,
Say; hell in fire, she sho' got 'nough, baby!

U—h, Lawd, ol' un bring in de meat,
U—h, Lawd, ol' un bring in de meat,
U—h, Lawd, ol' un bring in de meat,
Dis new gal of mine she got all de sweet, baby!

U—h, Lawdy, dem rations am good,
U—h, Lawdy, dem rations am good,
U—h, Lawdy, dem rations am good,
Have sech a good time, if de ol' woman would, baby!

Some o' Dese Days

Some o' dese days,
Hit won't be long,
Mammy gonna call me
An' I be gone.

Some o' dese nights,
An' I don't kere,
Mammy gonna want me
An' I won't be here.

Some o' dese days
In de by an' by,
You won't have no'n' t' eat,
Den you gonna cry.

Some o' dese days
While I's here to home,
Better feed me an' pet me,
Don't, I's gonna roam.

YOU TAKE DE STOCKIN', I TAKE DE SOCK

You take de stockin', I take de sock, honey,
You take de stockin', I take de sock, baby,
You take de stockin', I take de sock,
Take you all night to wind dat clock, honey.

You take de garter an' I take de string, honey,
You take de garter an' I take de string, baby,
You take de garter an' I take de string,
You gits de money, I don't git a thing, honey.

You take de slipper, I take de shoe, honey,
You take de slipper, I take de shoe, baby,
You take de slipper, I take de shoe,
I don't kere now whut you gonna do, honey.

You take de boot an' I take de laig, honey,
You take de boot an' I take de laig, baby,
You take de boot an' I take de laig,
You ain't nuffin but a rotten aig, honey.

PULL OFF DEM SHOES I BOUGHT YOU

A

Goin' up de country,
Dont' you wanta go?
Git me out my
Rag time clo'es.

Pull off dem shoes I bought you,
Pull off dem socks I bought you,
Pull off dat hat I bought you,
You know you have mistreated me.

Tore up all my clo'es;
Pull off dat wig I brung you,
Let yo' devilish head go bal'.

B

Mary, Mary, when I met you
You didn't have no clo'es at all.
Now I ax you kindly, Miss Mary,
Give me dem shoes, stockin's, an' dat petticoat,
An' dat dress an' hat, an' las' dat wig,
An' let yo' head go bal'.

Mammy-in-Law Done Turn Me Out

Keep on a-worryin',
What's it all about?
Mammy-in-law
Done turn me out.

Don't bring in no sugar,
Don't bring in no meat,
Don't never bring in
Nothin' to eat.
Mammy-in-law done turn me out.

Don't bring in no rations,
Don't bring in no dough,
'Nother man hang around her do'.
Mammy-in-law done turn me out.

De Women Don't Love Me No Mo'

De women don't love me no mo',
I's a broke man from po' man's town.
De women don't love me no mo',
'Cause I can't buy her stockin's an' a gown,
'Cause I can't buy her stockin's an' a gown.

I don't kere, don't matter wid me,
I don't love to work no mo'.
Got to have money, got to have clo'es,
Don't, a feller can't make no show.

De gal love de money
An' de man love de gal;
If dey bofe don't git what dey wants,
It's livin' in hell.

The Negro man runs true to masculine style when he philosophizes upon the subject of woman. Needless to say, his philosophy is often the result of his failure to get along with the other sex. When he is "down" on womankind the burden of his song is that woman is the cause of most of the trouble in the world. He avows that

Woman is a good thing an' a bad thing, too,
They quit in the wrong an' start out bran' new.

Or he declares that he will never again have anything
to do with women:

> All I hope in dis bright worl':
> If I love anybody, don't let it be a girl.

One of his strong points is giving advice to others in
order that they may avoid his mistakes. "Listen to
me, buddy," he says, "let me tell you what a woman 'll
do."

> Don't never git one woman on yo' min',
> Keep you in trouble all yo' time.

De Woman Am De Cause of It All and the songs immediately following it are typical of the songs of the
woman-hater. *Dey Got Each and de Other's Man* is
as clever a bit of cynicism as one could want.

DE WOMAN AM DE CAUSE OF IT ALL

A

> De woman am de cause of it all,
> De woman am de cause of it all,
> She's de cause of po' Adam's fall,
> De woman's de cause of it all.
>
> Bill and John fall jes' de same,
> Bill and John fall jes' de same,
> De onliest difference, dey ain't got po' Adam's name,
> But de woman am de cause of it all.
>
> She strips yo' pocket book,
> She strips yo' pocket book,
> Den tells de police you a damn crook,
> De woman am de cause of it all.
>
> Workin' in de gang, 'out no frien',
> Workin' in de gang, 'out no frien',
> Nobody comes, brings nuffin' in,
> De woman am de cause of it all.

B

De woman is de cause of it all,
She's de cause of Daddy Adam's fall.

Ol' Daddy Adam, Ol' Mudder Eve,
Takin' all dese years to bring in de sheaves.

Ol' Miss Eve didn't have no showin'
Widout heaps of stags to keep her goin'.

If dey'd been twenty stags in de Garden of Eden,
De devil and de sarpent sho'd got beaten.

If Dere's a Man in de Moon [1]

If dere's a man in de moon,
Dere's a woman hangin' roun'.
If dere's a man in de moon,
She nag at 'im, I be boun'.

Man in de moon, man in de moon,
Wonder if dat man's a coon,
Wonder if dat man's a coon,
Wonder if dat man's a coon,
Dat man in de moon.

Go fer a walkin' out at night,
See dat woman pickin' a fight.

Man in de moon, man in de moon,
Wonder if dat man am a coon,
Wonder if dat man am a coon,
Wonder if dat man am a coon,
Dat roun' face man in de moon.

A Vampire of Your Own

If you want to have a vampire of your own,
Let these loose women alone.
Fix up your wife you have at home,
An' you'll have a vampire of your own.

---

[1] Probably derived from the song *If the Man in the Moon Were a Coon,* which was a popular minstrel several years ago.

Stop spendin' your money on other women,
An' your friends, you have not any.
Go home at night, treat your own wife right,
An' you'll have a vampire of your own.

Dey Got Each and de Udder's Man

See two passenger trains, Lawd,
Runnin' side by side.
See two womens, see two womens,
Stan' an' talk so long.
Bet yo' life dey got
Each and de udder's man.

The Negro man is at his best when he sings of his "gal" or his "baby." Sometimes his song is boastful of the qualities of his "gal." Sometimes he compares the merits of the brown girl and the yellow girl or of the black and the yellow and casts his vote for his favorite color. Again, he sings the story of his courtship, and he counts it a never-to-be-too-much-talked-about experience to have been driven away from his sweetheart's house by an irate father. In *My Jane* the lover characterizes his "gal" with enviable terseness and humor.

My Jane

My Jane am a gal dat loves red shoes,
My Jane am a gal dat loves silk clo'es.

My Jane am a gal what loves plenty money,
She can devil a feller till it ain't even funny.

My Jane am a gal dat loves heaps o' men,
Gits what you got an' dat's yo' en'.

My Jane am a gal loves to frolic all night,
Won't cook fer a feller, not even a bite.

My Jane's a gal gits all she can,
If you ain't got it, she hunts another man.

My Jane am a gal drive a feller to de bad,
But Jane's, hell-o-mighty, bes' gal I ever had!

My Gal's a High Bo'n Lady

My gal she's a high bo'n lady,
She's dark but not too shady,
All de mens fall fer dat
    High bo'n gal o' mine!

Chorus:

She's a high bo'n baby,
She's a high bo'n lady,
She's a brown dat suits my eye.

De mens dey calls her cutie,
Dat gal a natural bo'n beauty,
All de same I's in de ring
    Fer dat high bo'n brown o' mine.

If You Want to See a Pretty Girl

Rubber is a pretty thing,
You rub it to make it shine.
If you want to see a pretty girl,
Take a peep at mine, take a peep at mine.

Talkin' about a pretty girl,
You jus' ought-a see mine.
She is not so pretty
But she is jus' so fine.

She gives me sugar,
She gives me lard,
She works all the while
In the white folks' yard.

Honey Baby

If I could lay my head on yo' sweet breas',
Honey baby, I could fin' sweet res'.
Sweet res', sweet res',
Honey baby, I could fin' sweet res'.

If I could set down in your lap,
Baby mine, I could have a nap.
Good nap, sweet nap,
Honey baby, I could have a nap.

GIVE ME A TEASIN' BROWN

If 'twant fer de ter'pin pie
And sto'-bought ham,
Dese country women
Couldn't git nowhere.

Some say, give me a high yaller,
I say, give me a teasin' brown,
For it takes a teasin' brown
To satisfy my soul.

For some folksies say
A yaller is low down,
But teasin' brown
Is what I's crazy about.

YOU TAKE DE YALLER, I TAKE DE BLACK

Yaller gal's yourn
An' de black gal's mine,
You never can tell
When de yaller gal's lyin'.

Give me a chocolate drop,
She's white on de inside,
Black on de back.
She don't cause a feller
To ride de railroad track.

You take yaller,
I take de black,
Hurry up, nigger,
Come out'n dat shack.

Dat chocolate
Gal am mine.

LONG, TALL, BROWN-SKIN GIRL

I'm Alabama boun',
Long, tall, brown-skin girl.
I'm Alabama boun',
I'm Alabama boun'.

I have a mule to ride
To that long, tall, brown-skin girl.
I have a mule to ride,
I have a mule to ride.

She is on the road somewhere,
She is a long, tall, brown-skin girl.
She is on the road somewhere,
She is on the road somewhere.

You can leave me here
With my long, tall, brown-skin girl.
You can leave me here,
You can leave me here.

I Got a Gal an' I Can't Git Her

I got a gal an' I can't git her,
I got a gal an' I can't git her,
I got a gal an' I can't git her,
Mammy won't lemme see 'er, can't even go wid her.

Went to de house, I wus lovin' sick,
Went to de house, I wus lovin' sick,
Went to de house, I wus lovin' sick,
I got over dat spell, Lawd, mighty quick.

Daddy had a pistol, mammy had a gun,
Daddy had a pistol, mammy had a gun,
Daddy had a pistol, mammy had a gun,
Totin' my stuff roun' de corner, Lawd, wus fun.

I Went to See My Gal

I went to see my gal at half pas' fo'
Her ol' fool daddy met me at de do'.

"I come to git a match," so says, says I.
"Write it on yo' tombstone, by and by."

I kicked up dirt, I kicked up san',
Lawd, I kicked up everything but dry lan'.

You ax me did I run?—No, Lawd, I flew.
I's a mighty black nigger, he skeered me blue.

BABY, WHY DON'T YOU TREAT ME RIGHT

I'm goin' down to the rivuh,
I'm goin' to jump overboard an' drown,
Because the girl I love,
I can't see her all the time.

Chorus:

Baby, why don't you treat me right,
So that I can love you all the night?
Then you will be my sweet little wife.
Baby, why don't you treat me right?

I'm coming to see you tomorrow night,
I want everything to be just right,
I'm coming to get my own,
An' I want that shine to leave you alone.

DEY'S HANGIN' 'ROUN' HER DO'

Dey's a-hangin' 'roun' her do',
Dey's never done dat befo',
Fer she's wearin' her aprons low.
Lawdy, Lawdy, I don't wanta go,
All dese niggers hang 'roun' her do',
'Cause she's wearin' 'em hangin' low.

Unfaithfulness in love is another great source of
song. "Somebody stole my gal" is a common tale,
and the sequel, "I'm gonna git dat man," is equally
common. The "creeper," the man who "fools wid
another man's woman," is the most despised of all
Negro characters. Says the Negro man,

A sarpent crawls on his belly,
A cat wallers on his back;
De meanest varmint in de worl'
Is de creeper in my shack.

In the following group of songs the man pays his
respects to the unfaithful woman and to the "creeper."

A Creeper's Been 'Roun' Dis Do'

You don't think I don't know
A creeper's been 'roun' dis do, dis do'.

A sarpent crawls on his belly,
A cat wallers on his back,
De meanest varmint in dis worl'
Is de creeper in my shack.

My woman say hit's her brother,
Den say hit's her daddy, too;
If dat midnight creeper don't stay 'way,
I know what I's gonna do.

My han's am long,
My fingers am strong and slim,
When I gits through wid dat creeper's neck
Dey won't be creeps lef' in him.

Dew-drop Mine

Keep me, sleep me, close on yo' heart,
Tell me, angel Susie, never mo' to part.
My black baby, you got no wings,
But, my black baby, you got better things.

Angel mine, you quit lyin'
In de bed wid dat udder man,
Dew-drop mine, I's a cryin'
Fer you, but I's spyin'.

Angel mine, dis I know,
You don't love me no mo'.
Dew-drop mine, dis I know,
A midnight creeper come in my do'.

He Tuck Her Away

I sho' got to fight, I's got to use de knife,
'Cause dat stray done got my wife.
Oh, he tuck her away, he tuck her away.

I Got My Man

Look out, nigger, hol' up yo' han'.
Waited long time, but I got my man.
You got de gal, I got you,
Devil git us bofe 'fore we gits through.

Home Again, Home Again [1]

Home again, home again,
Crazy to git back.
When I gets dere,
Finds a stray man in my shack,
Finds a stray man in my shack,
Finds a stray man in my shack,
Home again, home again,
Finds a stray man in my shack.

Home again, home again,
Axe handle in de yard,
Whales dat nigger over de head.
Now I's workin' hard,
Now I's workin' hard,
Now I's workin' hard,
Home again, home again,
Now I's workin' hard.

De chain gang got me, an' de coal mine, too,
But, Lawd, what's a po' nigger gonna do
When a creeper comes creepin' in,
When a creeper comes creepin' in,
When a creeper comes creepin' in?
Home again, home again,
When a creeper comes a-creepin' in.

I's Done Spot My Nigger

Han' on my gun,
Finger on de trigger,
I's goin' to jail
'Cause I's done spot my nigger.

[1] Cf. *Home Again Blues*, a popular phonograph piece.

My woman done fool me,
Everything gone wrong;
I ain't never gonna live
To sing dis song.

Jedge an' jury
Sentenced me to hang,
Jes' as lieve to go dere
As to go to de gang.

HE GOT MY GAL

Come up Whitehall,
Run out 'Catur,
I'se boun' fer to fin' dat
Big black waiter.

Chorus:

He got my gal, he got my gal,
He got my gal, he got my gal,
I boun' now to git dat man.

He give her money,
He give her fine wear;
But when I finds dat waiter,
Watch out fer his hair.

SHE'S GOT ANOTHER DADDY

Bill Snipe's wife couldn't buy no coffin,
But 'hin' her veil I seen her laughin'.
She's got another daddy, Lawd,
She's got another daddy.

Bill's wife rid 'hin' de hearse,
She rid in a hack,
I kotch her grinnin' at her new daddy
Out'n a crack.
She's got another daddy, Lawd,
She's got another daddy.

CHAPTER IX

WOMAN'S SONG OF MAN

Woman's song of man is in most respects parallel to man's song of woman. Her themes are about the same. She sings of her "man" or "daddy," of her disappointments and failures in love, of her unfaithful lover, and of her own secret amours.

It will be noticed that woman's song conforms quite closely to the blues type as it is popularly known today. In Chapter I examples of the "mama" blues titles were given and in Chapter II it was pointed out that the majority of the formal blues of today deal with the sex theme. Furthermore, most of these blues are sung from the point of view of woman. Consequently, as songs that may be remembered and sung from day to day, they appear more acceptable to woman than to man. Perhaps this explains why the influence of the formal blues is encountered so frequently in the kind of songs with which this chapter is concerned. At any rate, it is becoming increasingly difficult to find a song of woman on the man theme which does not show the influence of the popular blues. [1]

Woman's song of man frequently concerns itself with "the other woman," the rival in the case. The first two songs given here are only indirectly concerned with man, but they are of interest because they

[1] After consulting dozens of popular pieces, in both sheet music and phonograph record form, we have been able to trace some of these songs to them, but we feel sure that the influence of the formal blues is present in many other songs in this and other chapters, even though we have failed so far to locate the direct evidence. We have omitted many songs that were clearly of formal origin, although the singers insisted that they were entirely original.

touch upon the "conflict of color" within the Negro community. They are only samples of a voluminous literature of "chocolate" versus "yellow," or "black" versus "brown," which is to be found in the songs of the Negro.

De Mulatto Gal

De mulatto gal got yaller skin, yaller skin,
De mulatto gal got yaller skin, yaller skin,
De mulatto gal got yaller skin, yaller skin,
De mulatto gal got yaller skin,
Den she got a devilish grin, daddy.

De mulatto gal got kinky hair, kinky hair,
De mulatto gal got kinky hair, kinky hair,
De mulatto gal got kinky hair, kinky hair,
De mulatto gal got kinky hair,
Always wears her big laigs bare, daddy.

De mulatto gal got white-gray eyes, gray eyes,
De mulatto gal got white-gray eyes, gray eyes,
De mulatto gal got white-gray eyes, gray eyes,
De mulatto gal got white-gray eyes,
An' dat's a gal dat never lies, daddy.

De mulatto gal got great big laigs, big laigs,
De mulatto gal got great big laigs, big laigs,
De mulatto gal got great big laigs, big laigs,
De mulatto gal got great big laigs,
She's de gal makes de men beg, daddy.

De mulatto gal got great big hips, big hips,
De mulatto gal got great big hips, big hips,
De mulatto gal got great big hips, big hips,
De mulatto gal got great big hips,
She's de gal got kissin' lips, daddy.

De Chocolate Gal

De chocolate gal got greasy hair, greasy hair,
De chocolate gal got greasy hair, greasy hair,
De chocolate gal got greasy hair, greasy hair,
She is de gal can cuss an' rare, daddy.

De chocolate gal got col' black eye, black eye,
De chocolate gal got col' black eye, black eye,
De chocolate gal got col' black eye, black eye,
She am de gal what steals an' lies, daddy.

De chocolate gal got thick black skin, black skin,
De chocolate gal got thick black skin, black skin,
De chocolate gal got thick black skin, black skin,
She de kin' of gal what go to de pen, daddy.

De chocolate gal she got big laigs, big laigs,
De chocolate gal she got big laigs, big laigs,
De chocolate gal she got big laigs, big laigs,
She am de gal what cries an' begs, daddy.

De chocolate gal got heavy hips, heavy hips,
De chocolate gal got heavy hips, heavy hips,
De chocolate gal got heavy hips, heavy hips,
She's de gal got lyin' lips, daddy.

Songs like those just given are varied to suit the color of the singer. If the black girl has an off-color rival, she sings that it is the yellow girl who "steals an' lies," who "cries an' begs," who "can cuss an' rare," and so on.

In the next few songs woman sings of her "man." Her appellations, "my man," "my daddy," "sweet papa," "chocolate drop," "Black Jack," and others, are an interesting study in themselves. *I's Dreamin of You* has simplicity and a note of tenderness which approaches the better type of love song. The other songs are quite crude, but it should be remembered that they are characteristic only of the Negro woman of the lower class.

I's Dreamin' of You

I's dreamin' of you,
I's dreamin' of you,
I's dreamin' of you
Every night.

I's thinkin' of you,
I's thinkin' of you
I's thinkin' of you
All right.

I's wantin' of you,
I's wantin' of you,
I's wantin' of you
Day an' night.

On de Road Somewhere

On de road somewhere,
I got a long, tall chocolate-drop
On de road somewhere.
Don't you leave me here,
Don't you leave me here,
If you will leave me here,
Leave me dime fer beer.
On de road somewhere,
On de road somewhere,
I got a long, tall chocolate-drop
On de road somewhere.

My Black Jack

When I gits to heaven I don't wanta stay
Widout my Black Jack live out dat way.
Black Jack's a rounder, but I don't kere,
All us need to be happy is a bed an' a cheer.

Daddy Mine

Over de fiel' an' 'cross de line,
I got a daddy dat I call mine.
Daddy mine, daddy mine,
Keep me cryin' all de time.
Ain't got no heart, ain't got no mon,
But, God, I loves dat daddy lak fun.
Daddy mine, daddy mine,
I got a daddy dat I calls mine,
Daddy mine, daddy mine.

My Man Am a Slap-stick Man

My man am a slap-stick man,
My man dance wid de band.
His head am nappy,
His feetsies is long;
None o' dese things
Make my man wrong.
My man's a slap-stick man.

My man am a slap-stick man,
My man dance wid dat yaller gal.
Her head am nappy,
Her feet am long;
All o' dese things
Make dat gal dead wrong.
My man's de slap-stick man.

Don't You Two-time Me

If you gonna be my honey
Don't you two-time me.
If you gonna be my papa,
Better have one man 'stead of three.
Don't you two-time,
Try to two-time me.

Can Any One Take Sweet Mama's Place?[1]

Can any one take sweet mama's place?
I ain't good lookin',
Ain't got no curly hair,
But my mama give me somethin'
Take me each an' everywhere.
Come here, sweet papa,
Look me in de face,
Is dere anybody can take yo' mama's place?

De Mississippi River
Is so deep and wide,
Can't see my good brown
From de other side.

---

[1] Cf. phonograph record, *Can Anybody Take Sweet Mama's Place?*

But the chief theme in woman's song, as in man's, is trouble. Sometimes the dominant note is disappointment:

> Dat nigger o' mine don't love me no mo',
> Dat ungrateful feller don't love me no mo'.

Sometimes it is regret:

> I wish I was single again,
> Oh, I wish I was single again.

Again the key-note is one of despondency:

> Done sol' my soul to de devil,
> An' my heart done turned to stone.

And it is usually the "other woman" who is at the bottom of the trouble.

> He don't send me no hearin'—
> I knows another gal's dere an' I's fearin'.

> Dat sly, 'ceitful, lyin' gal,
> Yes, Lawd, she stole my man away.

These "hard luck" songs of woman are presented in the next group. It is here that one finds the closest relation between folk songs and the formal blues.

When I Wore My Ap'on Low

> When I wore my ap'on low,
> When I wore my ap'on low,
> When I wore my ap'on low,
> Boys would pass by my do'.

> Now I'm wearin' it to my chin,
> Now I'm wearin' it to my chin,
> Now I'm wearin' it to my chin,
> Boys all pass and dey won't come in.

I Done Sol' My Soul to de Devil [1]

I done sol' my soul,
Done sol' it to de devil,
An' my heart done turned to stone.
I got a lot o' gol',
Got it from de devil,
Because he won't let me alone.

He says he can make me happy
An' give me back my man
If you follow me in sin,
An' I wus so blue he took me in.
Look what a fool I am.

Done sol' my soul,
Done sol' it to the devil,
An' my heart done turned to stone.

I live down in de valley
By a hornet's nest,
Where de lions, bears, and tigers
Come to take deir rest.

I Got a Letter From My Man [2]

I got a letter from my man,
My man's dyin', Lawd, Lawd.

I'm goin' down track, never look back,
Goin' where my man fell dead.

I'm gonna follow my man,
Lawd, gonna follow him to the buryin' groun'.

But I'm so sorry, Lawd,
But I just can't take your place.

Well, captain, told you about my man,
Say, I'm goin' away, can't stay behind.

[1] Very similar to phonograph piece, *Done Sold My Soul to the Devil.*
[2] This song represents the lament of a construction-camp woman. The sentiment of the first four stanzas is found, in a very different form, in the phonograph piece, *Death Letter Blues.*

Say, I'm goin' away, captain,
Lawd, I done lef' this town.

Say, I'm goin' home, captain, an', captain,
I won't be here so long.

Say, I'm goin' away, Lawd, Lawd,
Say, I'm on my way home.

O Lawd, captain, tell me what's matter now,
Nothin' matter, jus' leavin' the town.

Captain, captain, I'm goin' away so long,
You make me think o' my man.

Say, captain, captain, don't be so hard on me,
O Lawd, I don't do nothin' but wash an' iron all day.

Say, captain, captain, I can't work so hard,
O Lawd, I can't wash an' iron so hard.

Say, captain, when you call my name,
You make me think, Lawd o' my man.

Say, captain, I ain't got no husban',
Lawd, captain, you got my man.

I Ain't No Stranger

I ain't no stranger,
I ain't no stranger,
I jes' blow into your town.
I didn't come here,
I didn't come here.
To be dawged around.
Look-a here, daddy,
Look-a here, daddy,
See what you done done.
Done made me love you,
Den tryin' to throw me away.

See dem crazy fellows, daddy?
Go to jail about 'em,
But I wont go in—

WHAT CAN THE MATTER BE?[1]

What can the matter be, O dear, what can the matter be?
What can the matter be, O dear, Johnnie is so long at
    the fair.
He promised to bring me a ring an' a locket
An' all the nice things you wear in your pocket.
He promised to bring me a bunch of blue ribbon
To wear on my pretty brown hair.

He said if I'd love him he never would leave me,
But now I have chased him I hope he won't grieve me,
I love him so dearly I hope he won't leave me,
But Johnnie is so long at the fair.
O dear, what can the matter be?
Johnnie is so long at the fair.

WORRIED ANYHOW[2]

When de man dat I love says
He didn't want me no mo',
I thought it was de hardest word
I ever heard befo'.

When de blues overtake you,
I's can't beat a deal,
If it wusn't fer my mother
An' de man I loves.

I give myself to de sick
An' my soul to de God above.
If you quit me, daddy,
It won't worry me now,
Because when we are together
I am worried anyhow.

---

[1] This song, which is probably of white origin, has a wide distribution.
The present version is from North Carolina. The song is mentioned in
Pound's syllabus, *Folk Song of Nebraska and the Central West.* Perrow
gives a version in *Journal of American Folk-Lore*, vol. 28, p. 169.
[2] Cf. phonograph record, *Worried Anyhow Blues.*

DERE'S MISERY IN DIS LAN'

I got a man an' a sweetheart, too,
I got a man an' a sweetheart, too,
I got a man an' a sweetheart, too,
Dere's misery in dis lan', dis lan'.

Can't please my man an' my sweetheart, too,
Can't please my man an' my sweetheart, too,
Can't please my man an' my sweetheart, too,
Dere's misery in dis lan', dis lan'.

My man makes money an' my sweetheart makes none,
My man makes money an' my sweetheart makes none,
My man makes money an' my sweetheart makes none,
Dere's misery in dis lan', dis lan'.

My sweetheart makes love an' my man makes none,
My sweetheart makes love an' my man makes none,
My sweetheart makes love an' my man makes none,
Dere's misery in dis lan', dis lan'.

DAT CHOCOLATE MAN

I ain't never goin' to be satisfied,
All day an' night I cried.
Dat big Bill o' mine he hide
From me, yes, from me.

My ol' haid it's weary,
My ol' heart it's dreary
For dat chocolate man.

I wonder where dat slim Bill's gone,
I can't do nothin' but set an' mo'n.
Dat big Bill stray from me,
Yes, he stray from me.

My bed it's lonesome an' col',
I can't sleep to save my soul.
Dat big Bill o' mine,
He's got dat yaller gal.

My ol' haid it's achin',
My ol' heart it's breakin'
For dat chocolate man.

Dem Longin', Wantin' Blues

I loves dat bully, he sho' looks good to me,
I always do what he wants me to.
Den he don't seem satisfied.
I got de blues,
Yes, Saro, I's got dem wantin' blues,
Dem longin', wantin' blues.

He don't send me no hearin',
I know another gal's dere an' I's fearin'.
He don't seem satisfied.
Now I got de blues,
Yes, Lawd, I got dem wantin' blues,
Dem longin', wantin' blues.

Dat Nigger o' Mine Don't Love Me No Mo'.

Up an' down de street, ain't got no show,
Dat nigger o' mine don't love me no mo'.

No mo', no mo', no show, no show,
'Cause dat ungrateful feller don't love me no mo'.

Stroll to de corner, cop in sight,
Gonna kill dat man, he ain't treat me right.

No mo', no mo', no show, no show,
'Cause dat ungrateful feller don't love me no mo'.

I Don't Love Him No Mo'.

If I don't come back,
If I don't come back,
Put de cop on dat
Black man's track.

He's a rough-neck black,
Keep de p'liceman on his track,
Put 'im in de jail house,
Keep 'im dere.
I don't love him no mo',
So I don't care.

I Wish I Was Single Again [1]

When I was single I was livin' at my ease,
Now I am married a drunker to please.
I wish I was single again,
I wish I was single again.

When I was single, fine shoes I wo',
Now I am married, my feet on the flo'.
I wish I was single again,
I wish I was single again.

The water is to bring, the flo' to sweep,
The children are cryin' and nothin' to eat.
I wish I was single again,
I wish I was single again.

Wash their little faces, tuck them in their bed,
In comes that drunken man—I wish he was dead.
I wish I was single again,
I wish I was single again.

Dere's a Lizzie After My Man

Dere's a Lizzie after my man,
Dere's a Lizzie after my man;
She git 'im if she can,
'Cause I kotch her holdin' his han',
Dis-a mawnin', dis evenin' more 'n late.

Her face am powdered white,
Her face am powdered white;
Her hair am greasy an' slick,
On my man she try to work 'er trick,
Dis-a mawnin', dis evenin' more 'n soon.

She comed 'roun' to my do',
She comed 'roun' to my do';
Den I ripped offen her skirt,
Den I tore offen his shirt,
Dis-a mawnin', dis evenin', more 'n soon.

---

[1] Cf. Campbell & Sharp, *English Folk Songs from the Southern Appalachians*, p. 256; also phonograph record version, *I Wish I Was a Single Girl*.

Dat Sly Gal

Dat sly gal,
Oh, dat sly, 'ceitful, lyin' gal,
She leads dat long tearful prayer
Wid her head propped on my chair.
She stole my man away,
Yes, Lawd, she stole my man away.

I Don't Feel Welcome Here

I's goin' down de road
Where I can get better care.
I believe I'll go
'Cause I don't feel welcome here.

I's goin' to ketch dat train,
Dont' kere where it's from,
'Cause I ain't gonna stay here
An' be made no stumblin' block.

I landed here one night
When de clock wus strikin' nine,
Lookin' fer dat woman
Dat had stole dat man o' mine.

I hunts dat woman high,
I hunts dat woman low,
I's gonna rip dat woman
From her mouf clean down befo'.

Occupied

Coon, coon, coon, great big yaller coon,
He sets all night jis' outern my do'.
He says, "Please lemme res' dere jis' once mo',"
But, Lawd, it's occupied,
But, Lawd, it's occupied.

Dat coon'd be hot if he knowed de troof,
Dat a chocolate-drop lef' over de roof.
But he wanta come in once mo'
An' be occupied,
An' be occupied.

I'm Gonna Get Me Another Man

My man ain't treatin' me right,
He haven't been home this week.
I'm goin' get me another man
An' let that black kinky-headed bastard go.
He don't love me an' he don't mean me no good.

I'm a brown-skin woman an' tailor-made,
I believe I can get me a man in anybody's town.
The man I love an' am wild about,
He is brown-skin,
Got curled hair an' tailor-made hisself.

I Got Another Daddy

Leavin' here, I sho' don't wanta go.
Goin' up de country,
Brown-skin, I can't carry you.

Don't write me no letters,
Dont' sen' me no word,
I got another daddy
To take your place.

CHAPTER X

FOLK MINSTREL TYPES

ONE of the most interesting of all the Negro's secular songs is the folk minstrel type. This minstrel song is similar to the original minstrel, in which one or more wandering musicians and songsters travel from place to place rendering song and music with varied accompaniments. Sometimes one singer goes alone, sometimes two, sometimes a quartette. They are entertainers in the real sense that they exhibit themselves and their art with all the naturalness and spontaneity possible. Furthermore, such minstrels are not infrequently ingenious in composing new verses and adapting them to old tunes or to newly discovered ones. Such songs are also well adapted to social gatherings and to various special occasions. They should be distinguished from the black-face type of vaudeville song and the minstrel show, although of course the song of the traveling show must inevitably influence the minstrel type a great deal. For sheer type-portraiture, however, the minstrel Negro and his song must undoubtedly be presented if the whole picture is to be complete.

Typical scenes are the singing on special gala occasions, such as fairs, holidays, and picnics, at resorts of the whites, on the road or on street corners. Such singers also accompany many a patent-medicine man or other street-corner vender of wares. Sung in this way, of course, are many of the ordinary secular creations, but in general the minstrel type is more finished and formal, with more of rhyme and something of the ballad technique, with much of the humor and entertaining qualities implied in its kind. Most of these songs would repay special study on the part of the student of folk songs and ballads who wishes to trace origins and developments. While all the songs we have listed are Negro songs in the sense that they are sung much and regularly by Negroes, with the special artistic expression and manner common to them, they are, of course, often much mixed with similar songs originating elsewhere. In the case of *It Ain't Gonna Rain No Mo'*, [1] for instance, the origin of course is a common one, and many of the scores of verses are sung alike by white and Negro minstrels, with only minor distinctions due to manner and situation. And yet of the several hundred verses which are even now extant, some are very clearly of Negro origin, exhibiting something of the Negro's traditional phrases and his blues. A Negro quartette singing *It Ain't Gonna Rain No Mo'* is undoubtedly singing a Negro song. Among the songs in the previous volume which are adapted to the minstrel type of singing are *Railroad Bill, Lilly, Stagolee, Eddy Jones*, [2] and some of the more recently composed religious types.

One of the most attractive of all the Negro songs we have heard was *That Liar*, sung by two elderly Negro men at Columbia, South Carolina, through the courtesy of Dr. E. L. C. Adams. The main part of the song is always chanted by the leader in recitative sing-song very much after the fashion of a sermon when the minister has reached his emotional climax. Then upon reaching the chorus, he suddenly turns into rapid

---

[1] No verses of *It Ain't Gonna Rain No Mo'* are given in this volume, although our collection included several score. They are scarcely within the bounds of the present collection.

[2] See *The Negro and His Songs*, pp. 196, 198, 205, 228.

song, accompanied by his companion. They sing
the chorus with the usual accompaniment of "Oh"
or "Lawd" or "Let me tell you." The song, with
some variations and repetitions, is good for almost an
hour's entertainment. It is also a very good shouting
song.

THAT LIAR [1]

Jes' let me tell you how a liar will do.
Always comin' with somethin' new,
He'll steal yo' heart with false pretense,
Makin' out like he's yo' bes' frien;
An' when he finds out you believe what he say,
Then that liar gonna have his way.
He'll bring you news 'bout women and men,
Make you fall out with yo' bes' frien'.

Chorus:

If you don't want to get in trouble,
If you don't want to get in trouble,
If you don't want to get in trouble,
You better let that liar alone.

When a liar takes a notion his friends to improve,
He lay around de neighbors and git de news.
Nearly every day when yu look out,
See that liar come to yo' house,
Tell you sich lies surprise yo' min'
An' mix a little truth to make it shine.
An' when he git his news fix jes' right,
That liar gonna cause a fight.

When everything's in perfect peace,
Here come that liar with his deceit,
Make believe that he love you so well,
Till every day he must come an' tell.
"Let me tell you, my sister, if you jes' knew
What a certain somebody tell me 'bout you."
He studies up lie and tell it so smooth,
Until you think undoubtedly must be true.
He'll bring you out to trace de tale,
An' if you don't mind you'll be put in jail.

---

[1] Cf. The song given by Ballanta in his *St. Helena Island Spirituals*, p. 72.

A hypocrite and liar both keep up a fuss,
Dey both very bad, but a liar's the wuss;
He'll come to yo' house in powerful rush,
Say, "I can't stay long for I must go to my work,
I jes' come to tell you what somebody say."
Then he'll take a seat an' stay all day.
He'll tell you some things that'll cause you to pout,
Then at las' he'll force you out.
He knows that he owes you, an' if you ask him for pay,
He'll fall out wid you and stay away.

Sung in very much the same way is the *War Jubilee Song*, itself a type of popular traveling song. It was the favorite of the same two singers, both noted songsters of the Columbia environs, and they claimed to have learned it from a traveling Negro secretary of the Y. W. C. A., who came from Florida immediately after the World War. Here again the chorus was sung with effective variations, "Now I'm so glad," or "You know I'm so glad," or "I declare I'm so glad," and many others.

WAR JUBILEE SONG

When the U. S. got in de war
Wus de saddes' day I ever saw.
Registration day began to start
An' it come near breakin' all mothers' heart.

Chorus:

Now I'm so glad, I'm so glad,
Now I'm so glad, I'm so glad,
Now I'm so glad, I'm so glad
Jesus brought peace all over dis lan'.
You know, I declare,
Jesus brought peace all over dis lan'.

But God who called us here below
Tol' de boys, "Get ready, with you I'll go."
Jes' take me over in Germany lan'
An' I will conquer every man.

When time fer train to roll,
Uncle Sam had boys under his control,
An' when town bell begin to ring
Some tried to be happy and begin to sing.

Some from Newport News, so I am tol',
An' some in France where it was col'.
Jes' carry me over in de lan' of France
Where every soldier will have a fightin' chance.

That vessel leave New York with thousands on board,
Steam ship carry such a heavy load.
Lawd, I'm over in very strange lan',
Wid all soldiers walk han' in han'.

An' no good Christian did not fear,
'Cause Jesus Christ was engineer,
Engineer standin' at chariot wheel
Backin' up children on battle fiel'.

Reason why war did last so long,
So many people was livin' wrong,
Jes' goin' round runnin' down colors and race
An' oughter been beggin' fer little mo' grace.

Whilst dey wus fightin' great noise wus heard,
Smoke wus flyin' jes' lak a bird,
Men were dyin' wid thousands of groans,
Now peace declared an' boys at home.

Uncle Sam he made and signed a decree
For American nation to ben' de knee.
God sits in Heaven an' answers prayer,
An' dey had to stop fightin' over there.

We put ourselves as debt to God,
We say we'd follow where he trod,
But de way got dark and we couldn't see
Jes' who de winner of war would be.

But de Christians prayed until dey cried,
Hypocrite say dat dey had lied.
But in deir heads dey had a doubt,
But when peace was declared, Lawd, dey wanted to
  shout.

One of the most entertaining songs in all the repertoire of the Negro's aggregate creations is *Mr. Epting*,
sung by four Negro pick-and-shovel men with such
zest and harmony as we have rarely heard. It is
apparently a parody on the war song *Good Morning,
Mr. Zip*, and with this particular quartette of workers
would make a hit on any stage. In the singing, the
largest member of the group dances a jig and exclaims
in his big bass voice, "Lawd, Lawd, I feels funny
when I sings this song. Lawd, Lawd, I can't keep
still, it gives me such a funny feelin'. Whoopee!
Singin' 'bout white man gives me funny feelin'." In
addition to the verses sung here the singer may sub-
titute for whiskey and cocaine such words as gun,
woman, policeman, work, and other forces which may
be calculated to lead to the demise of these slanderers
of Mr. Epting.

GOOD MORNING, MR. EPTING

Good morning, Mr. Epting,
Your hair just nappy as mine.
Good morning, Mr. Epting,
You belong to the K. K. kind.
Well, ashes to ashes,
Well, dust to dust,
Show me a woman
That you can trust.
Good morning, Mr. Epting,
Your hair just nappy as mine.

Good morning, Mr. Epting,
Your hair just kinky as mine.
Good morning, Mr. Epting,
You belong to the K. K. kind.
Well, ashes to ashes,
Well, dust to dust,
Show me a woman
That you can trust.
Good morning, Mr. Epting,
Your hair just kinky as mine.

Good morning, Mr. Epting,
Your hair just as black as mine.
Good morning, Mr. Epting,
You belong to the K. K. kind.
Well, if whiskey don't kill me,
Well, cocaine must,
Show me a woman
That you can trust.
Good morning, Mr. Epting,
Your hair just black as mine.

Good morning, Mr. Epting,
Your hair just black as mine.
Good morning, Mr. Epting,
You belong to the K. K. kind.
Pistol don't kill me,
Well, cocaine must,
Show me a woman
That you can trust.
Good morning, Mr. Epting,
Your hair just as black as mine.

Good morning, Mr. Epting,
Your hair just short as mine.
Good morning, Mr. Epting,
You belong to the K. K. kind.
Well if whiskey don't kill me,
Well, cocaine must,
Show me a woman
That you can trust.
Good morning, Mr. Epting,
Your hair just as short as mine.

The old song *Raise a Rukus Tonight* is now a popular one in various forms, those given here representing Georgia, Tennessee and North Carolina. There are many other versions and fragments, but these will suffice to indicate the type and mixture so common at present. One may easily see the similarity to the old song but also its corruption by such modern types as *It Ain't Gonna Rain No Mo'*. *Wring Jing*, while not a "rukus" chorus, is so much of the same sort as to make its comparison of value. The other much varied and corrupted types are also valuable for comparative purposes.

RAISE A RUKUS TONIGHT

A

My ol' master promise me,
Raise rukus tonight;
Before he died he'd set me free,
Raise rukus tonight.

Chorus:

Come along, chillun, come along,
While the moon is shining bright,
Get on board, down the river float,
'Cause we gonna raise a rukus tonight.

His hair come out and his head turned bal',
Raise rukus tonight;
He got out o' notion dyin' at all,
Raise rukus tonight.

'Scuse me, mister, don't get mad,
Raise rukus tonight;
'Cause you look like sumpin the buzzards had,
Raise rukus tonight.

Look at that nigger, ain't he black?
Raise rukus tonight;
Got hair on his head like a carpet tack,
Raise rukus tonight.

Black cat settin' on chimney jam,
Raise rukus tonight;
If that ain't hot place, I'll be damn,
Raise rukus tonight.

Way down yonder on chit'lin' switch,
Raise rukus tonight;
Bull frog jump from ditch to ditch,
Raise rukus tonight.

Bull frog jump from bottom of well,
Raise rukus tonight;
Swore, by God, he jumped from hell,
Raise rukus tonight.

RAISE A RUKUS TONIGHT

B

Some folks say preacher won't steal,
Raise rukus tonight;
I caught two in my corn fiel',
Raise rukus tonight.

One had a bushel, one had fo',
Raise rukus tonight;
If that ain't stealin' I don't know,
Raise rukus tonight.

My ol' missus promised me,
Raise rukus tonight;
When she died she'd set me free,
Raise rukus tonight.

She live so long 'til she got bal',
Raise rukus tonight;
She got out notion dyin' at all,
Raise rukus tonight.

So come along, chillun, come along,
Where moon shine bright tonight;
Get on board before boat gone,
Gonna raise rukus tonight.

RAISE A RUKUS TONIGHT

C

Come on, niggers,
While the moon is shining bright,
Get on the boat,
Down the river we'll float,
We're gonna raise a rukus tonight.

Come on, little chillun,
While the moon is shining bright,

We're gonna raise cornbread
An' sweet potatoes tonight,
Raise rukus tonight.

My ol' missus promised me,
Raise rukus tonight,
When she died she'd set me free.
We're gonna raise a rukus tonight,
Gonna raise a rukus tonight.

My ol' master promised me,
Gonna raise a rukus tonight,
When I grew to be a man
He'd give me a horse's rein.
Gonna raise a rukus tonight.

WRING JING HAD A LITTLE DING

If I live to see next fall,
Wring Jing had a little ding,
Ain't goin' to have no lover at all,
Wring Jing had a little ding.
My ol' missus promised me,
Wring Jing had a little ding,
When she died she'd set me free,
Wring Jing, had a little ding.

When she died she died so po',
Wring Jing had a little ding,
She left me sittin' on de kitchen flo',
Wring Jing had a little ding.
Bull frog jumped into bottom of well,
Wring Jing had a little 'ding,
Swore, by golly, he jumped in hell,
Wring Jing had a little ding.

My ol' missus had a mule,
Wring Jing had a little ding,
His name was Martin Brown,
Wring Jing had a little ding.
Every foot that Martin had,
Wring Jing had a little ding,
Would cover an acre of groun',
Wring Jing had a little ding.

GWINE TO GIT A HOME BY AN' BY

My ol' missus promised me,
Gwine to git a home by an' by,
When she died, she'd set me free,
Gwine to git a home by an' by.
She did live till she got bal',
Gwine to git a home by an' by,
And she never died at all,
Gwine to git a home by an' by.

Chorus:

Den O dat watermelon!
Lamb of goodness, you must die;
I'm gwine to jine de contraband, chillun,
Gwine to git a home by an' by.

A shoo-fly cut a pigeon wing,
Gwine to git a home by an' by;
A rattlesnake rolled in a 'possum's skin,
Gwine to git a home by an' by.
Cow path crooked gwine through the wood,
Gwine to git a home by an' by,
Missus says I shan't, I says I should,
Gwine to git a home by an' by.

Sister Sue and ol' Aunt Sallie,
Gwine to git a home by an' by,
Both live down in shin-bone alley,
Gwine to git a home by an' by.
Name on de house, name on de do',
Gwine to git a home by an' by,
Big green spot on de grocery sto',
Gwine to git a home by an' by.

There are many songs of the mule, some of which are old and being revived, some of which have been made new by the phonograph records. The first illustration here was sung with remarkable effect at the Dayton, Tennessee, Scopes trial, with hundreds of whites and Negroes standing around the quartette of Negroes

who came for the occasion. Most of their songs were
of the stereotyped sort, such as *Ain't Gonna Rain No
Mo'*. The mule song is the best illustration of the
minstrel type given in this volume. The other mule
songs are presented largely for comparison, and are
not particularly valuable. One of these, exhorting
Miss Liza to keep her seat, is similar to the version
collected twenty years ago in Mississippi. [1]

Go 'Long Mule

I've got a mule, he's such a fool
He never pays no heed;
I built a fire 'neath his tail,
An' then he showed some speed.

Chorus:

Go 'long, mule,
Don't you roll dem eyes;
You can change a fool, but a doggone mule
Is a mule until he dies.

Drove down to the graveyard,
Some peaceful rest to fin';
But when a black cat crossed my path
I sure did change my min'.

My gal's ol' man don't like me much,
He's got a heart o' flint;
Last night I saw him buy a gun
An' I can take a hint.

I bought some biscuits for my dog
An' put them on the shelf;
Times got so hard I shot the dog
An' ate them up myself.

Both Rufus Akes an' Rastus Payne
Got married down in Gaines;
An' now they say the Georgia woods
Are full of Akes an' Paynes.

[1] See *The Negro and His Songs*, p. 235.

A cowslip ain't no kind o' slip
To slip upon a cow;
That's why a catfish never answers
To a cat's meow.

A man in Georgia pulled a gun
An' took a shot at me;
Just as he took the second shot
I passed through Tennessee.

Bill Jones was taken ill while callin'
On his gal Salome.
What really caused his illness was
Her husband who came home.

They say some one's been stealin' things,
It's kind-a newsed aroun';
I swear I don't know who it is,
But I am leavin' town.

I'm goin' to the river now
To lay me down and die,
An' if I find the water's wet
I'll wait until it's dry.

My gal invited me to dine,
I went prepared to eat;
But all she placed upon my plate
Was chicken necks and feet.

They're gonna hold a meetin' there
Of some society.
There's 'leven sheets upon the line,
That's ten too much for me. [1]

---

[1] Evidently refers to a Ku Klux Klan meeting.

HUMP-BACK MULE

If you want to sneeze,
Tell you what to do,
Get some salt an' pepper,
Put it in yo' shoe.
Ridin' hump-back mule,
Ridin' hump-back mule,
If you want to see pretty yaller gal,
She's ridin' a hump-back mule.

Ol' massa bought pretty yaller gal,
Bought her from the South,
She wrapped her hair so tight
She couldn't open her mouth.
Ridin' hump-back mule,
Ridin' hump-back mule,
If you want to see pretty yaller gal,
She's ridin' a hump-back mule.

Carried her to blacksmith shop
To have her mouth made small,
She back her years and open her mouth
An' swallowed shop and all.
Ridin' hump-back mule,
Ridin' hump-back mule,
If you want to see pretty yaller gal,
She's ridin' a hump-back mule.

Niggers plant de cotton on hill,
Niggers pick it out,
White man pocket money,
Nigger does without.
Ridin' hump-back mule,
Ridin' hump-back mule,
If you want to see pretty yaller gal,
She's ridin' a hump-back mule.

WHOA, MULE

I hear dem sleigh bells ringin', snow am fallin' fas',
I's got dis mule in de horness, got him hitched at las'.
Liza, get yo' bonnet, come an' take a seat,
Grab up dat robe you're sittin' on an' cover up yo' feet.

Chorus:

Whoa, mule, whoa I say!
Keep yo' seat, Miss Liza Jane, an' hold on to de sleigh.
Whoa, mule, whoa I say!
Keep yo' seat, Miss Liza Jane, an' hold on to de sleigh.

What's dis mule a-roamin' for? He ain't got half a load.
When you catch dis mule a-roamin', jus' give him all
    de road.
Don't get scared at nothin', you stay here today,
Liza, help me hold dis mule, or else he'll get away.

Watch dis mule a-goin', goodness how he can sail!
Watch his big ears floppin', see him sling his tail.
Goin' down to de 'possum, Liza, you keep cool,
I ain't got time to kiss you now, I's busy with dis mule.

A NIGGER'S HARD TO FOOL

A Georgia nigger an' a Georgia mule,
Dese two asses is hard to fool.
Might fool a white man,
Might fool his mother,
Might fool his sister,
An' you might fool his brother;
But a nigger's hard to fool,
But a nigger's hard to fool.

A Georgia yaller gal
An' a Georgia black
Kin always dog
A feller's track,
But he's hard to fool.
Yes, Lawd, a nigger's hard to fool.

A Georgia road's red,
Bottom lan' black,
A Georgia nigger
Is a cracker jack,
An' he's hard to fool.
Yes, Lawd, a nigger's hard to fool.

I'm Fishin' Boun'

Look 'cross the fiel', see the sun comin' down,
Dis is de day to be layin' 'roun'.
Bait in de can, hook on de stick,
I'm done too lazy to hit a lick,
I'm fishin' boun', I'm fishin' boun'.

Lazies got me, an' I don't keer,
Stomach's empty, but who's gonna fear?
Bait in de can, hook on de stick,
Fishin' spell done got me, I can't hit a lick,
I'm fishin' boun', I'm fishin' boun'.

Come on fellers, wid yo' luck in yo' han'
We's gonna eat minners out de fryin' pan,
Bait in de can, hook on de line,
If I don't go to fishin', nigger, I'll be dyin',
I'm fishin' boun', I'm fishin' boun.

Stretch flat on yo' belly wid yo' back in de air,
Look out fo' yo' hook, Lawd, he's bitin' dere!
Bait in de can, hook on de stick,
I'm plum' so hungry, I'm most nigh sick,
I'm fishin' boun', I'm fishin' boun'.

Co'n Bread

Co'n bread, co'n bread,
Feed dis nigger on co'n bread.

White man eats biscuit,
Nigger eats pone;
Nigger he's de stronges'
Jes' sho's you bo'n.

Co'n bread, co'n bread,
Give dis nigger greasy co'n bread.

Put on de skillit,
Po' in de grease,
Don't make a little,
But a great big piece.

Co'n bread, co'n bread,
All lazy niggers loves co'n bread.

Sif' out de bran an'
Drap in de pone,
Lawd knowed whut he's doin'
When he made dat co'n.

Co'n bread, co'n bread,
Give dis nigger plenty co'n bread.

You loves Emma an'
I loves Jake.
You is de nigger
Some greasy co'n bread to bake.

Co'n bread, co'n bread,
Black greasy nigger eats co'n bread.

One han' in de hopper,
De udder in de sack,
Ol' black nigger wid
Red lips to smack.

Co'n bread, co'n bread,
Black greasy nigger eats co'n bread.

'Taters in de hill,
Meal in de bag,
Home-made sirup
In de old black keg.

Co'n bread, co'n bread,
Black lazy nigger eats co'n bread.

Ashes in de corner,
Fire in de middle;
Woman cooks rations,
Man sets an' whittles.

Co'n bread, co'n bread,
Feed dis nigger on co'n bread.

Other songs which are current through the singing of the minstrel type, or distributed widely on printed sheets in much the same way as the "mule" songs, are *No Coon But You, De Co't House in De Sky,* and

Hi-Jenny-Ho, sent us by Mr. J. D. Arthur of Tennessee. The *Pullman Porter* is a little more sophisticated, but represents a type of humor and easy-going vaudeville style.

No Coon But You

As I was strollin' down the street,
  "Who did you meet?"
A yellah gal I chanced to meet.
  "What did you say?"
Said I, "My little honey, now who's
  you gwine to meet?
May I have the pleasure of walkin'
  down the street
With the one I long so for?   You are
  the apple of my eye."
An' then she turned her sparklin' eyes
  an' quickly said to me:

Chorus:

"No coon but you, babe, no coon but you,
No coon but you, babe, will ever do.
No coon but you, babe, no coon but you,
No coon but you will ever do."

As we were passin' down the street,
  "What happened then?"
Her Sunday babe we chanced to meet.
  "What happened then?"
He grabbed me by the shoulder, he quickly
  turned me 'roun'.
Said I, "Look out here, nigger, I'll fall
  you to the groun'."
But he took away my yellah gal, an' as
  they passed me by,
I heard him say, "Now who's your babe?" an'
  then she said to him:

"No coon but you, babe," *etc.*

That very same night there was a ball.
   "Where, nigger, where?"
Down at the Black Fo'-Hundred's Hall,
   "S'pose you were there?"
Yes, I took along my razuh, an' gave
   it such a swing,
I cut that yellah nigger right under
   his left wing.
An' as they carried out his corpse
   I heard the people say,
"Now who'll be her babe?" an' then
   she said to me:

"No coon but you, babe," *etc.*

DE CO'T HOUSE IN DE SKY

I's got a notion in my head
As when you come to die,
You'll stand a 'zamination
In de co't house in de sky.
You'll be astonished at the questions
That the angels gwine to ax,
When they get you on the witness stan'
An' pin you to the facts.
Den yo' eyes will open wider
Than they ever done befo',
When they ax you 'bout the chicken scrapes
What happened long ago.

Chorus:

To de co't house in de sky
I will raise my wings an' fly,
An' stan' the 'zamination
In de co't house in de sky.

Now de angels on de picket line
Along the milky way
Keeps watchin' what you're doin'
An' hearin' what you say.
No matter what you're gwine to do,
No matter whar you're gwine,
They's mighty apt to find it out
An' pass it long de line.

Den often in de meetin'-house
You make a fuss or laugh,
Den the news it goes a kitin'
'Long the golden telegraph.
Den de angel in de office,
What is settin' by the gate,
Jes' reads the message with a look
An' claps it on de slate.

Oh, you'd better do yo' duty, boys,
An' keep yo' conscience clear,
An' keep a-lookin' straight ahead
An' watchin' whar you steer.
'Cause after while the time will come
To journey from dis lan',
Dey'll take you 'way up in de air
An' place you on de stan'.
Den you'll have to listen mighty close
An' answer mighty straight,
If you ever 'spects to enter
Through that pretty golden gate.
Oh, you'd better stop yo' foolin',
That's a place you can't slide by,
When you stan' the 'zamination
In de co't house in de sky.

HI, JENNY, HO, JENNY JOHNSON

Once I loved a yaller gal, she said she'd marry me,
Hi, Jenny, ho, Jenny, ho, my Jenny Johnson!
Saw her eatin' apples at a huckleberry bee,
Hi, Jenny, ho, Jenny Johnson!
Took her to a ball an' we never did get back
Till the break of morn, when you hear the chickens
    quack.
She wouldn't take the cars, so I took her in a hack;
Hi, Jenny, ho, Jenny Johnson!

Chorus:

Hi, Jenny, ho, Jenny, come along with me,
Hi, Jenny, ho, Jenny, ho, my Jenny Johnson!
Sweeter than the honey at a huckleberry bee,
Hi, Jenny, ho, Jenny Johnson!

O my darling Jenny, she's the sweetest girl in town,
Hi, Jenny, ho, Jenny, ho, my Jenny Johnson!
Captivates the neighborhood for miles an' miles aroun',
Hi, Jenny, ho, Jenny Johnson!
Said she loved another an' it broke my heart in two,
An' I had to get it mended with a little piece of glue;
She gave me back my locket an' a little silver shoe,
Hi, Jenny, ho, Jenny Johnson!

Now my Jenny's married to a little yaller coon,
Hi, Jenny, ho, Jenny, ho, my Jenny Johnson!
Take care for Jenny's hubby, for he'll kill you mighty
   soon,
Hi, Jenny, ho, Jenny Johnson!
Wooly-headed pickaninnies runnin' roun' the flo',
For they say there's only two, but I wish they had a sco';
I'm gwine away to China, so I'll never see her mo',
Hi, Jenny, ho, Jenny Johnson!

PULLMAN PORTER

Runs from California
Plumb up to Maine.
I's a Negro porter
On de pullman train.
   Pullman train,
   Pullman train,
I's de Negro porter
On de pullman train.

Braid on the cap an'
Buttons in a row,
On that blue uniform
Right down the fo'.
   In pullman train,
   Pullman train,
I's a Negro porter
On de pullman train.

It's a tip right here
An' a tip right thar,
Tip all along
Up an' down de pullman car.

Pullman train,
Pullman train,
I's a Negro porter
On de pullman train.

Pocket full o' money,
Stomach full o' feed,
What next in the worl'
Do a fellow need?
    Pullman train,
    Pullman train,
I's a Negro porter
On de pullman train.

Kitty Kimo [1]

Dar was a frog lived in a spring,
He had such a cold dat he could not sing,
I pulled him out an' frowed him on de groun',
Ol' frog he bounced an' run aroun'.

Chorus:

Camo, kimo, daro, war,
My high, my ho, my rumstipumstididdle,
Soot bag, pidly-wickem, linch 'em, nip cat,
Sing song, Polly, won't you kime, oh?

Milk in de dairy, nine days ol',
Rats an' skippers are gettin' hol';
A long-tailed rat in a bucket of souse,
Jes' come from de white folks' house.

In North Carolina de niggers grow,
If de white man only plant his toe.
Water de ground with 'bacco smoke,
An' up de nigger's head will poke.

Way down South in Cedar street,
Dere's where de niggers grow ten feet,
Dey go to bed, but 'tain't no use,
Deir feet hang out for a chicken's roos'.

---

[1] Cf. Scarborough, *On the Trail of Negro Folk-Songs*, pp. 156-7.

CHAPTER XI

WORKADAY RELIGIOUS SONGS

M ANY a laborer, although singing his full quota of
secular songs, still finds his workaday solace
best in his favorite heritage of church and religious
melodies.   There is surcease of sorrow in the plaintive

> Yes, Lawd, burden down, burden down,
> O Lawd, since I laid my burden down.

And the appeal for relief from present difficulties, so
eloquently expressed in the previous chapters, finds its
counterpart in this favorite of many workers of the
present day.

> Do, Lawd, remember me,
> Do, Lawd, remember me,
> When I'm in trouble,
> Do, Lawd, remember me.
>
> When I'm low down,
> Do, Lawd, remember me.
> Oh, when I'm low down,
> Do, Lawd, remember me.
>
> Don't have no cross,
> Do, Lawd, remember me,
> Don't have no crown,
> Do, Lawd, remember me.

There seems to be an impression abroad to the effect
that the making of Negro spirituals stopped long ago.
On the contrary, it is quite probable that more spirituals
are being made today than during the days of slavery.
As a matter of fact the old spirituals have never been

static. It is no longer possible to speak of the "pure" or "original" version of *Swing Low, Sweet Chariot*, of *Roll, Jordan, Roll*, or any other of the old favorites. If any one is in doubt of this, let him compare the words and music of the spirituals as they were recorded by Allen and others in 1867 with the records of the same songs later made by Fenner and Work and with the recent versions in James Weldon Johnson's *Book of American Negro Spirituals*. Or let him compare the songs as they are sung at Hampton with the same songs as they are sung at Tuskegee or at Fisk. The spirituals, like all other folk songs, are dynamic. Sometimes in the process of constant change there appear variations which are so unlike the parent songs as to constitute virtually new songs. In this way the old spirituals have been the inspiration for untold numbers of new religious songs.

Among the lowly Negro folk of the South the making of spirituals is still a reality. Every community has its "composers." Often they are supposed to possess some special gift of the "spirit." From sermon, prayer, and crude folk wisdom they draw ideas and inspiration for their compositions. Sometimes the results are pathetic, but not infrequently there springs up a song which would compare favorably with the old spirituals.

It is not the purpose of this chapter to present the old spirituals or merely their newer variations, but rather to give some of the more unsophisticated religious songs of the workaday Negro as they are sung today in the South, by the same groups and individuals whose songs and verbal pictures this volume presents. They are not the kind of songs which are usually sung in the Negro churches, for many of them have only individual or local significance, while others show distinct secular touches.

Biblical themes continue to find a place in the Negro's religious songs. Moses and Pharaoh and Noah and the ark are still the favorites. Here are a few of the workaday religious songs now current in the South. *Pharaoh's Army Got Drownded* is a favorite with children, and is often sung by them as a sort of reel. The three songs following it were sung by a woman in Georgia who is known locally as Sanctified Mary Harris. She claims that they are her own compositions and says that she composes only when she in "under de spirit."

PHARAOH'S ARMY GOT DROWNDED

Mary, don't you weep an', Marthie, don't you moan,
Mary, don't you weep an', Marthie, don't you moan;
Pharaoh's army got drownded,
O baby, don't you weep.

I thinks every day an' I wish I could
Stan' on de rock whar Moses stood;
Oh, Pharaoh's army got drownded,
O baby, don't you weep.

If you git dere befo' I do,
Tell de Cap'n I's a-comin' too;
Pharaoh's army got drownded,
O baby, don't you weep.

If I had wings lak de angels have,
I never be caught drivin' in anudder cab;
Pharaoh's army got drownded,
O baby, don't you weep.

Baby, don't you weep an', baby, don't you moan,
You has to go to heaven wid yo' buryin' clothes on;
Pharaoh's army got drownded,
O baby, don't you weep.

Gonna Turn Back Pharoah's Army

When de children wus in bondage
Dey cried unto de Lawd,
"O turn back Pharaoh's army."
Hallelu!

Chorus:

Gonna turn back Pharaoh's army,
Hallelu!
Yes, a-gonna turn back Pharaoh's army,
Hallelu!

I write to Marse Jesus
To send some valiant solders
Jus' to turn back Pharaoh's army,
Hallelu!

When Moses smit de water
The children all cross over,
Den dey turn back Pharaoh's army,
Hallelu!

Didn't Ol' Pharaoh Get Lost?

God spoke to Moses, "Pharaoh now,
Fer I have harden Pharaoh's heart to me,
Fer he will not bow."

Chorus:

Didn't ol' Pharaoh get lost, get lost!
Didn't ol' Pharaoh get lost in de Red Sea?

Moses went unto Pharaoh
An' did whut de Lawd said how,
But God had harden Pharaoh's heart,
He would not let dem go.

Who Built de Ark?

De very fust thing dat Nora done,
He cut this timber down.
De very next thing dat Nora done
He huded it all aroun'.

Chorus:

Who built de ark?   Nora, Nora.
Who built de ark?   Nora an' his Lawd.
Who built de ark?   Nora, Nora.
Who built de ark?   Nora an' his Lawd.

Nora said to de rovin' bird,
"Go bring me a grain of san'."
De rovin' bird cried, "O Lawd,
I can't find no lan'."

The old songs had much to say about trouble, the struggle with sin and the devil, and the warning to the sinner man. Favorite lines used to be:

Nobody knows de trouble I've seen

I'm a-rollin' through an unfriendly worl'

O my good Lawd, keep me from sinkin' down

We are climbin' Jacob's ladder

My sins so heavy I can't get along

Sinner, what you gonna do?

O sinner, don't you let dis harves' pass

Perhaps Satan and the terrors of hell and judgment are not pictured as frequently and as vividly as they used to be, but they are still a vital part of Negro song. The following songs portray the struggle with sin, the warning to the sinner, and the superior status of the sanctified as opposed to the sinner.

GOOD LAWD, I AM TROUBLED

Troubles makes me weep an' moan,
Goin' where troubles be no mo';
Good Lawd, I am troubled.

Troubles meet me at de do',
Goin' where troubles be no mo';
Good Lawd, I am troubled.

Troubles up and troubles down,
Troubles never makes me frown;
Good Lawd, I am troubled.

We Will Kneel 'Roun' de Altar

Lawd, help me to be mo' humble,
Lawd, help me to be mo' humble,
In dat great gittin'-up mornin',
Lawd, help me be mo' humble in dis worl'.

Chorus:

We will kneel 'roun' de altar on our knees,
We will kneel 'roun' de altar on our knees,
We will kneel 'roun' de altar
Till we view de risin' sun.
O Lawd, have mercy on me.

Lawd, help me be mo' faithful,
Lawd, help me be mo' faithful in dis worl'.
We will see God's risin' sun,
Lawd, help me be mo' humble in dis worl'.

Lawd, help de widders an' de orphans in dis worl',
Lawd, help de widders an' de orphans in dis worl'.
In dis great gittin'-up mawnin',
Lawd, help the widders an' de orphans in dis worl'.

De Devil's Been to My House [1]

De devil's been to my house today, today,
De devil's been to my house today, today,
Lawd, de devil's been to my house today, today,
De devil's been to my house today, today.

I kicked him out my do' today, today,
I kicked him out my do' today, today,
Lawd, I kicked him out my do' today, today,
I kicked him out my do' today, today.

---

[1] The next three songs are compositions of Sanctified Mary Harris. *Have Everlastin' Life* has little originality, however.

I's goin' sin-huntin' today, today,
I's goin' sin-huntin' today, today,
Lawd, I's goin' sin-huntin' today, today,
I's goin' sin-huntin' today, today.

JES' BEHOL' WHAT A NUMBER!

Yonder comes my sister
Who I's loves so well.
By her disobedience
She have made her bed in hell.

Chorus:

Jes' behol' what a number!
Jes' behol' what a number!
Jes' behol' what a number
From every grave-yard.

I looks unto de eas',
I looks unto de wes',
I see de dead a-risin'
From every grave-yard.

HAVE EVERLASTIN' LIFE

Better min', my sister, how you walk on de cross,
Have on everlastin' life,
Your foot might slip an' your soul get los',
Have everlastin' life.

Chorus:

Oh, he dat believe, oh, he dat believe,
He shall have on everlastin' life.
He dat believe on de father an' de son
Shall have everlastin' life.

De tallest tree in paradise,
Have everlastin' life,
De Christian call it de tree of life,
Put on everlastin' life.

The Sanctified

Say, who's gonna ride my father's horse?
Say, who's gonna ride my father's horse?
Say, who's gonna ride my father's horse?
   Thank God, the sanctified.

Say, none can ride but the sanctified,
Say, none can ride but the sanctified,
Say, none can ride but the sanctified,
   Thank God, the sanctified.

Say, Paul he rode with the sanctified,
Say, Paul he rode with the sanctified,
Say, Paul he rode with the sanctified,
   Thank God, the sanctified.

No sinner rides with the sanctified,
No sinner rides with the sanctified,
No sinner rides with the sanctified,
   Thank God, I'm sanctified.

What You Gonna Do?

Sinner, what you gonna do
When de world's on fi-er?
Sinner, what you gonna do
When de world's on fi-er?
Sinner, what you gonna do
When de world's on fi-er?
O my Lawd.

Brother, what you gonna do? *etc.*

Sister, what you gonna do? *etc.*

Father, what you gonna do? *etc.*

Mother, what you gonna do? *etc.*

I Love Jesus

Dark was de night an' cold was de groun'
On which de Lawd had laid;
Drops of sweat run down,
In agony he prayed.

Would thou despise my bleedin' lam'
An' choose de way to hell,
Still steppin' down to de tomb,
An' yet prepared no mo'?

I love Jesus,
I love Jesus,
I love Jesus,
O yes, I do,
Yes, Lawdy.

SAVE ME, LAWD

Lawd, have mercy, Lawd, have mercy.
Lawd, have mercy, Lawd, have mercy.
Save po' me,
Save po' sinner,
Save po' sinner,
Save po' sinner,
Save me, Lawd.

I am a-dyin',
I am a-dyin',
I am a-dyin',
Save me, Lawd.

O Lawd, bless me, O Lawd, bless me,
O Lawd, bless me, O Lawd, bless me.
Save po' me,
Save po' sinner,
Save po' sinner,
Save po' sinner,
Save me, Lawd.

Parting and death are the subjects of the saddest songs that the Negro sings. The following songs awaken thoughts of the old folk saying their goodby's at the last service of a revival meeting or parting after a long-hoped-for family reunion. *I Bid You a Long Farewell* is one of the favorites of Aunt Georgia Victrum, age eighty-three, of Jasper County, Georgia.

I Bid You a Long Farewell

Mother, meetin' is over,
Mother, we mus' part.
If I never see you no mo',
I love you in my heart.

Chorus:

I bid you a long farewell,
Brother, I bid you a long farewell.
If I never see you no mo'
I bid you a las' farewell.

Brother, meetin' is over,
Brother, we must part.
If I never see you no mo',
I love you in my heart.

I Don't Want You All to Grieve After Me

I don't want you all to grieve after me,
I don't want you all to grieve after me.
Oh, when I'm dead an' buried in my col' silent tomb,
I don't want you all to grieve after me.

An' I will walk through the valley in peace,
An' I will walk through the valley in peace.
Oh, when I'm dead an' buried in my col', silent tomb,
I don't want you all to grieve after me.

My dear mother, don't you grieve after me,
My dear mother, don't you grieve after me.
Oh, when I'm dead an' buried in my col', silent tomb,
I don't want you all to grieve after me.

My ol' uncle, don't you grieve after me, *etc.* [1]

When I's Dead an' Gone

He is a dyin'-bed maker.
Jesus met a woman at de well,
An' she went runnin' home
An' tol' her friends,
"A man tol' me all I ever done."

---

[1] And so on for father, sister, brother, *etc., etc.*

The friends dey come a runnin' with de woman,
Saw Jesus settin' on de well,
He said he could give de livin' water
An' save yo' soul from hell.

He is a dyin'-bed maker.
When I's dead an' gone
Somebody gonna say I's lost,
But dey ought-a go down by Jordan
An' see whar Jesus led me 'cross.

When I's dead an' gone,
I don't want you to cry;
Jus' go on down to de ol' church
An' close my dyin' eye.

When Jesus hangin' on de cross,
His mudder began to moan.
He looked at his dear 'ciples
An say, "Take my dear mudder home."

Angels Lookin' at Me

Dig my grave wid a silver spade,
Angels lookin' at me.
Oh, look-a dere, look-a dere,
Oh, look-a dere, look-a dere,
Angels lookin' at me.

Drive me dere in a cerriage fine,
Angels lookin' at me.
Oh, look-a dere, look-a dere,
Oh, look-a dere, look-a dere,
Angels lookin' at me.

Let me down wid a silver chain,
Angels lookin' at me, *etc.*

All dem sinners can moan an' weep,
Angels lookin' at me, *etc.*

I's settin' in heaven in a golden cheer,
Angels lookin' at me, *etc.*

You Mus' Shroud My Body

Pray, mother, pray fer me,
Pray, Lawd, until I die.
You mus' shroud my body, Lawd,
An' lay it away.

Chorus:

I hear Jerusalem moan,
You mus' shroud my body, Lawd,
An' lay it away.

Pray, sister, pray fer me,
Pray, Lawd, until I die,
You mus' shroud my body, Lawd,
An' lay it away.

But death holds no terror for the Negro. He maintains that death's stream "chills the body but not the soul," and he believes that

’Way up in the Rock of Ages
In God's bosom gonna be my pillah.

As of old, heaven is the greatest theme of his religious song. He used to sing:

When I git to heaven gonna ease, ease,
Me an' my God gonna do as we please.

Now wait till I gits my gospel shoes,
Gonna walk about heaven an' spread the news.

Dere's a long white robe in de heaven for me.

No more hard trials in de kingdom.

Gonna feast off milk an' honey.

Now he sings:

I wants to go to heaven, set in de angel's seat;
I wants to go to heaven, eat what de angels eat.

I's gonna be in my home in heaven
When I lay my burden down.

I'm swingin' in de swinger,
Gonna swing me home to heaven.

I's gonna bathe my weary soul in paradise.

But let the songs speak for themselves. Among them
are some which might now be famous if they had only
been born seventy years ago.

I NEVER WILL TURN BACK

Jesus my all to heaven is gone,
I never will turn back
While de heaven's in my view,
He who I fix my heart upon.
I never will turn back
While heaven's in my view.

Chorus:

I never will,
I never will,
I never will turn back
While de heaven's in my view.

While de heaven's in my view
My journey I prosue.
I never will turn back
When heaven's in my view.

WHEN I LAY MY BURDEN DOWN

Glory, glory, hallelujah, when I lay my burden down,
Glory, glory, hallelujah, when I lay my burden down,
Glory, glory, hallelujah, when I lay my burden down,
I gonna be in heaven when I lay my burden down.

Glory, glory, hallelujah, I's goin' to my home on high,
Glory, glory, hallelujah, I's goin' to my home on high,
Glory, glory, hallelujah, I's goin' to my home on high,
I's gonna be in my home in heaven when I lay my burden
down.

SINCE I LAID MY BURDEN DOWN

I been shoutin',
I been shoutin'
Since I laid my burden down;
I been shoutin',
I been shoutin'
Since I laid my burden down.

Chorus:

Glory, glory, hallelujah,
Since I laid my burden down;
Glory, glory, hallelujah,
Since I laid my burden down.

I been prayerin',
I been prayerin'
Since I laid my burden down;
I been prayerin',
I been prayerin'
Since I laid my burden down.

IN DE MORNIN' SOON

Sister Sal she got on her travelin' shoes,
In de mornin' soon,
In de mornin' soon,
In de mornin' soon.
Yes, I's goin' to bury my weary soul
In de mornin' soon.

Sinners, I hates to leave you here,
Sinners, I hates to leave you here,
Sinners, I hates to leave you here,
'Cause I goin' to go to paradise
In de mornin' soon.

Some o' dese days jes' about noon,
Some o' dese days jes' about noon,
Some o' dese days jes' about noon,
I's goin' to bathe my weary soul in paradise
In de mornin' soon.

Oh, de Gospel Train's A-Comin'

Oh, de gospel train's a-comin',
Goodby, good by, good by.
Oh, de gospel train's a-comin',
Goodby.

Oh, de gospel train's a-comin',
Oh, de gospel train's a-comin',
Oh, de gospel train's a-comin',
Goodby.

Oh, she's comin' 'roun' de curve,
Goodby, good by, good by.
Oh, she's comin' ' roun' de curve,
Goodby.

Oh, de train am heavy loaded, *etc.*

Oh, sinner have you got you ticket? *etc.*

Oh, she's boun' straight way to heaven, *etc.*

Can't you change you way o' livin? *etc.*

Oh, Marse Jesus am de captain, *etc.*

Oh, de ride am free to heaven, *etc.*

Some o' These Days

I'm a-goin' to cross that river Jordan,
I'm a-goin' to cross that river Jordan, hal-lu-yah!
I'm a-goin' to cross that river Jordan,
I'm a-goin' to cross that river Jordan some o' these days.

I'm a-goin' to sit down side o' my Jesus,
I'm a-goin' to sit down side o' my Jesus, hal-lu-yah!
I'm a-goin' to sit down side o' my Jesus,
I'm a-goin' to sit down side o' my Jesus some o' these
days.

I'm a-goin' to tell him how I love him,
I'm a-goin' to tell him how I love him, hal-lu-yah!
I'm a-goin' to tell him how I love him,
I'm a-goin' to tell him how I love him some o' these
days.

I'm a-goin' to wear them golden slippers,
I'm a-goin' to wear them golden slippers, hal-lu-yah!
I'm a-goin' to wear them golden slippers,
I'm a-goin' to wear them golden slippers some o' these
    days.

I Wants to Go to Heaven

I wants to go to heaven,
Jine de angels' ban';
I wants to go to heaven,
Stan' where de angels stan'.

I wants to go to heaven,
Have some angel wing;
I wants to go to heaven,
See de Jesus King

I wants to go to heaven,
Shout lak de angels shout;
I wants to go to heaven
An' walk about.

I wants to go to heaven,
Set in de angels' seat;
I wants to go to heaven,
Eat what de angels eat.

I wants to go to heaven,
Weep when de angels weep;
I wants to go to heaven
Sleep where de angels sleep.

When I Git Home

Gonna shout trouble over
When I git home,
Gonna shout trouble over
When I git home.

No mo' prayin', no mo' dyin'
When I git home,
No mo' prayin' an' no mo' dyin'
When I git home.

Meet my father
When I git home.
Meet my father
When I git home.

Shake glad hands
When I git home,
Shake glad hands
When I git home.

Meet King Jesus
When I git home,
Yes, I meets King Jesus
When I git home.

I's Gonna Shine

I's gonna shine
Whiter dan snow,
When I gits to heaven
An' dey meets me at de do'.

Oh, shine, I will shine,
How dey shine, glory shine,
When I gits to heaven
An' dey meets me at de do'.

Shine, God a'-mighty shine,
All de sinners shine in de row;
But I'll be de out-shinedest
When dey meets me at de do'.

Oh, shine, de brudders shine,
Dey sisters shine ever mo',
When we all gits to heaven
An' dey meets us at de do'.

I's Swingin' in de Swinger [1]

I's swingin' in de swinger,
Thank God.
I's swingin' in de swinger,
Thank God.

---

[1] The idea for this novel song probably came from *Swing Low, Sweet Chariot*. It is another composition of Sanctified Mary Harris, as are also the two remaining songs in this chapter.

It's a bran' new swinger,
Thank God.
It's a bran' new swinger,
Thank God,
Thank God.

Goin' to swing me to heaven,
Thank God.
Goin' to swing me to heaven,
Thank God,
Thank God.

King Jesus in de swinger,
Thank God.
King Jesus in de swinger,
Thank God,
Thank God.

Goodby, Sing Hallelu

Goodby to sin an' sorrow,
Goodby, sing hallelu.

Farewell, sinner, I see you no mo',
Goodby, sing hallelu.

Goodby, hypocrite, you Beelzebub,
Goodby, sing hallelu.

I'm goin' away, I'll meet you in heaven,
Goodby, sing hallelu.

Farewell, mother, I meet you in de mawnin',
Goodby, sing hallelu.

I Calls My Jesus King Emanuel

O King Emanuel,
I calls my Jesus King Emanuel.

King Emanuel, he's a mighty 'Manuel,
I calls my Jesus King Emanuel.

Some calls him Jesus,
But I call my Jesus King Emanuel.

Because his power so great and strong,
I calls my Jesus King Emanuel.

CHAPTER XII

THE ANNALS AND BLUES OF
LEFT WING GORDON

HERE is a construction camp which employs largely Negro workers. In four years 8,504 laborers were employed and there was an average labor turnover of once each month, or forty-eight different sets of men working on the buildings and road under construction during that time. This camp employed men from different Southern states in the order named: North Carolina, South Carolina, Virginia, Tennessee, Georgia, Florida, Alabama, Texas, Mississippi, Louisiana; while stragglers represented eleven states outside the South. Why this turnover? Why do men travel from state to state? Of what sort are they? How many road camps and construction groups throughout the South duplicate this record? What are the experience, history, difficulties of the Negro worker by the roadside? Why does he quit his job? Where will he go for the next?

The entire story of the casual laborer will, of course, have to be told elsewhere in thorough studies of migration and case studies of many individuals. It is a remarkable story, sometimes unbelievable. It is not the purpose of this chapter to go into the matter of causes, but to present a picture of the workaday songster as a sort of cumulative example of the whole story of this volume. It is true that his early home life, his training, his experience, his relation to the whites, have all influenced him greatly. It is true also that there is often slack work, poor conditions of housing and work, little recreation, small wages, and always a

call to some better place. But we are concerned with
these here only as they are a part of the background of
the picture. Here is a type perhaps more representative of the Negro common man than any other. Now
a youngster of eight, father and mother dead, off to
Texas to an uncle, then—"po' mistreated boy"—he
goes to Louisiana, then to Mississippi, then to Georgia,
across South Carolina, back home to North Carolina,
then off to Philadelphia, to Pittsburg, to Ohio, to
Chicago, then back to the East and Harlem and back
South again. He is typical of a part of the Negro
movement of the decade. But there is continuously a
stream of moving laborers from country to town, from
town to town, from city to city, from state to state,
from South to North. Here is hardship, but withal
adventure, romance, and blind urge for survival.

As an example of this worker and songster we
present John Wesley Gordon, alias Left Wing [1] Gordon,
commonly called "Wing." He is very real, and one
could scarcely imagine a better summary of the
lonesome road, if made to order. Recent popular
volumes portraying the *species hobo* show no wanderers
arrayed like these black men of the lonesome road.
Walt Whitman's

> Afoot and light-hearted I take to the open road
> Healthy and free, the world before me,
> The long brown path before me, leading wherever I
>   choose

would seem a gentle taunt to Left Wing Gordon on the
red roads of Georgia or on the Seaboard rods in "sweet
ol' Alabam'." He had, at the last writing, given
excellent tale of working, loafing, singing his way

---

[1] So called because he had lost his right arm.

through thirty-eight states of the union, with such experience and adventure as would make a white man an epic hero. "You see, boss, I started travelin' when I wus 'leven years ol' an' now I'll be thirty this comin' August 26th. I didn't have no father an' mother, so I jes' started somewheres. I'd work fer folks, an' they wouldn't treat me right, so I moved on. An', Lawd, cap'n, I ain't stopped yet." And so he hadn't, for when on the morrow we came to put the finishing touches on his story, a fellow laborer said, "Law', boss, Wing done gone to Philadelphia."

"Wing," who started from St. Joseph in Missouri, lost his arm at eighteen years of age. He gives the following concrete data about some of the places where he has worked and loafed. What story might have been written if we had taken the states alphabetically, asking him for full details, with plenty of time, one can only imagine. Here is the order in which he volunteered information about the different states, in the geography of which he appears to be something of a scholar. The phraseology belongs to Wing and the inconsistencies remain as in his Iliad.

Louisiana. Worked on boat some an' saw-mill some.

Florida. Worked on hard roads.

Alabama. Worked in steel plants six miles from Birmingham.

Texas. Didn't do nothin' in Texas, had a little money to spend.

Arkansas. Worked at H——Hotel at New Port, fellow runnin' name Jack N——.

Missouri. Worked on boat.

Illinois. Sold papers in Chicago, started mowin' lawns, white-washin' fences, brushin' furniture, an' worked in packin' house.

Wyoming. Had a little money in Cheyenne an' didn't have nothin' to do.

Nebraska. At Omaha worked at packin' house.

Iowa. Worked in mines and on railroad.

Canada. Worked at government camp 'cross from Detroit, an' broom factory at Montreal.

Michigan. Worked at Ford factory at district on P. & M. railroad out north of Detroit.

Kansas. In harvest fields 'bout 37 miles from Leavenworth—Naw sir, never been in Leavenworth prisons.

North Carolina. On a job.

Arizona. Didn't do nothin' much.

South Carolina. On hard roads an' Southern Power Company.

Georgia. Comin' in a hurry, never fooled 'round there much. Did work in saw mill eight miles out from Waycross two weeks.

Tennessee. Out at Knoxville and Maysville at maloominum plant.

Mississippi. In boats at Vicksburg and Natchez.

Virginia. Worked most everywhere—Richmond at Broad Meadows, 1227 Brook Avenue.

New York. Out at Bessemer plants stirrin' pots.

Washington. At Alexandria, Virginia side.

Ohio. Worked for Mayor of Bridgeport, named C. J—.

West Virginia. At coal mines.

Pennsylvania. Worked in Pittsburg steel mills eight miles from Pittsburg.

Maryland. I's in Baltimore, had boat carry us out an' bring us back, Double A flashlight factory at 47 cents a hour.

New Jersey. Cross from New York, four miles from Nooark, work on Hansack River.

Wisconsin. Used to work out o' Milwaukee, butler on C. B. & Q. road; eight miles out but we stayed in Milwaukee.

Connecticut. Used to ketch boat an' go over to New Haven, Hartford, Thomasville, eight miles out from Springfiel', Massachusetts.

Massachusetts. Springfiel' and Boston, too. Didn't work none in Boston but had sister there.

Rhode Island. Never stopped there but I could walk all over that little state. Hartford is capital.

North Dakota. Wiped up engine on Great Northern, 237 miles from Minneapolis.

South Dakota. Worked out in Aberdeen in wheat fields, harvest for Al T——, mostly carried water.

California. When war was goin' on, time of government camp at Los Angeles an' Sacramento an' Miles City.

Wing was also a great songster. "When de 'Wing Blues' come out, dat's me," he would say. His chief refrain was always

> O my babe, you don't know my min',
> When you see me laughin',
> Laughin' to keep from cryin', [1]

of which he had many versions. This chorus was easily adapted to a hundred songs and varied accordingly. "When you see me laughin', I'm laughin' just to keep from cryin'," or "I'm tryin' to keep from cryin'," or "When you think I'm laughin', I'm cryin' all the time." There were his other versions, such as

> O my babe, you don't know my min',
> When you think I'm lovin' you
> I'm leavin' you behin',

with its similar variety, such as "I'm leavin' to worry you off my min'," or "When you think I'm leavin'

---

[1] One of the most popular blues today is a piece called *You Don't Know My Mind Blues.* We have evidence, however, which tends to show that numerous vulgar versions of the same title were current among the Negroes long before the formal song was published.

I'm comin' right behin'." Wing claimed a "Blues" for every state and more; if there was none already at hand, he would make one of his own. There were the various Southern blues, the *Boll Weevil Blues, Cornfield Blues, Gulf Coast Blues, Atlanta Blues, Alabama Blues, Birmingham Blues, Mississippi Blues, Louisiana Low Down, Shreveport Blues, New Orleans Wiggle, Norfolk Blues, Virginia Blues, Oklahoma Blues, Memphis Blues, Wabash Blues, St. Louis Blues, Carolina Blues, Charleston Blues*, and many others.

It must be admitted that Wing's blues were mixed and of wonderful proportions. He could sing almost any number of blues, fairly representative of the published type, with, of course, the typical additions, variations, and adaptations to time and occasion.

> Ohio, Ohio, West Virgini, too,
> De blues dis nigger's had only very few.
> What you gonna do?
> Lawd, what you gonna do?

> When I come from New York,
> Walkin' 'long the way,
> People pick me up
> Jes' to get me to pay,
> Ain't my place to live,
> Anyway you can't stay here.

> O Illinois Central,
> What can you spare?
> Fo' my baby's in trouble
> An' I ain't dere.
> Hey, Lawdy, Lawdy, I got crazy blues,
> Can't keep from cryin',
> Thinkin' about that baby o' mine.

> Lawd, I woke up dis mornin',
> Found my baby gone,
> Missed her from rollin'
> An' tumblin' in my arms.

O Lawd, if I feel tomorrow
Lak I feel to-day,
Good God, gonna pack my suitcase,
Lawd, an' walk away.

I'd rather be in jail,
Standin' like a log,
Than be here
Treated like a dog.

Creek's all muddy.
Pond's gone dry,
I never miss my baby
Till she said goodby.

Well, I went to graveyard
An' looked in my baby's face,
Said, "I love you, sweet baby,
Jes' can't take yo' place."

Whistle blowed on,
Church bell softly toned;
Well, I had good woman
But po' girl dead an' gone.

Well, I woke up dis mornin',
Had blues all 'round my bed;
I believe to my soul
Blues gonna kill me dead.

O baby, you don't know my min'.
When you think I'm laughin',
Laughin' to keep from cryin',
Laughin' to keep from cryin'.

Wing called that the *Louisiana Blues*, and certainly for the time being it was so. And for Georgia, although in his narrative he had given the Empire State of the South the usual Negro reputation of quick passage, he sang a mixed blues.

Dear ol' Georgia, my heart is sinkin'
An' my way come blinkin' to you,
If you ever leave Georgia any length o' time,
Yo' heart come blinkin', no other way but you,
Can't be no other way. [1]

Then for Alabama, Tennessee, Florida, California,
Virginia, there were other fragments, besides numerous formal versions.

Alabama, Tennessee,
I wrote my mother letter.
Don't write back to me,
Reason I tell you, I got de 'fo'-day blues.

I got de Florida blues,
Hey, mama, hey, baby, I got de crazy blues,
Hey, baby, you don't know my min',
When you think I'm leavin', I'm comin' all the time.

I ain't got no money,
No place to stay.
Hey, baby, hey, honey.
I got de Florida blues.

I got Elgin watch
Made on yo' frame.
Hey, baby, hey, honey,
I got Florida blues.

California ridden,
Don't think I'm didden,
De reason I'm tellin' you,
I have no place to stay.

Mother an' father dead,
Done gone away,
I'm a lonesome boy,
Got nowhere to stay.

---

[1] This and many other of Wing's stanzas have no clear meaning as far as
we can tell. Sometimes his songs give the impression that he has learned the
titles of numerous popular blues and has woven as many of them as possible
into each stanza.

Hey, mama, hey, baby,
I got de 'fo'-day blues.
I'm California ridden,
I got de California blues.

California in U. S.,
Dat is where my love lie,
An' she will treat me best,
You all take Alexander for ol' plaything,
But Alexander no name for you.
O baby, you don't know my min',
When you think I'm lovin' you, I'm leavin' you behin'.

Before continuing Left Wing's story, giving something more of the scope of his adventures, perhaps the best further introduction will be the exact record of some of his songs in the order in which he gave them. Wing had practically no variation in his tunes and technique of singing. A high-pitched voice, varied with occasional low tones, was the most important part of his repertoire. But what variation in words and scenes, phrases and verses, the recording of which would exhaust the time and endurance of the listener and call for an ever-recording instrument! For certainly the effort to transcribe everything Wing gave left the visitor amazingly exhausted, marveling at the jumbled resourcefulness of the singer, wishing for some new type of photography which would register the voice, looks, experience, and inimitable temperament of this itinerant camp follower.

Anna yo' peaches, but I's yo' man.
How I wonder where you goin' to-day,
That my mother an' father have nowhere to stay.
Would you take them in, oh, would you take them in?

How I love you, how I love you,
Would you take me in, would you take me in?
Anna yo' peaches, but I's yo man,
Would you take me in, would you take me in?

Lawd, I woke up dis mornin',
Couldn't keep from cryin',
Thinkin' about that
Lovin' babe o' mine.

O my babe, you don't know my min',
O you don't know my min'.
When you think I'm laughin',
I'm cryin' all de time.

Reason I love you so,
'Cause my heart is true,
Reason I love you so,
I'm goin' 'way.

I'm goin' 'way to worry you off my min'.
Reason I think you worry,
I'm 'way all the time,
I got de 'fo'-day blues.

You put yo' coat on yo' shoulder,
You want to walk away,
You got yo' lovin' baby,
You want a place to stay.

Well, I love you, baby,
God knows I do.
Reason I love you,
Yo' heart is true.
Reason I love you,
Got de weary blues.

Differing slightly in tone, Wing sets out on a new song only to swing back again to the same lonesome blues; indeed he makes his technique and his whines as he goes, the result blending into a remarkable product.

Eddy Studow been here,
You got de so long well,
'Cause I feel you sinkin',
Easin' down to hell,
O sweet baby, you don't know my min',
'Cause when you think I'm laughin', I'm cryin'.

If you don't b'lieve I'm sinkin',
Jes' look what a hole I'm in.
If you don't b'lieve I love you,
Jes' look what a fool I been.
O sweet baby, you don't know my min'.
When you think I'm lovin' you, I'm leavin' you behin'.

O baby, jes' ship my clo'es out in valise,
O baby, jes' ship my clo'es out in valise.
Reason I tell you ship 'em,
Yo' heart I don't believe.

Thought I woke up yesterday,
My heart was very sick,
'Cause reason I love you.
'Day's nearer pay day.

The reason I love my lovin' baby so,
Oh, reason I love my lovin' baby so,
'Cause if she make five dollars
She sho' bring her father fo'.

Yes, it's hey, sweet baby,
You don't know my min'.
'Cause it's hey, sweet baby.
You don't know my min'.
When you think I'm laughin',
Laughin' jes' to keep from cryin'.

O Lawd, what you gonna say,
I need de woman for de money,
I got no place to stay.
For de reason I love my lovin' baby so,
When she make eight dollahs,
Sho' bring her father fo'.

Ruther see you dead,
Floatin' in yo' grave;
Ruther see you dead,
Lawd, floatin' in yo' grave.
Than be here, Lawd,
Treated dis a-way.

Geech had my woman
An' two or three mo';
Oh, de Geech had my woman
An' two or three mo'.
He's a hard headed man
An' won't let me go.

I wake up dis mornin',
Feet half-way out de bed,
Lawd, I wake up dis mornin',
Oh, de blues you give me
Sho' gonna kill me dead.

Left Wing's story of his wanderings does not omit, of course, the woman part of his "lovin' worl'." Try as he might to sing of other experiences, inevitably he would swing back to his old theme.

I ruther be dead
In six feet o' clay,
Than to see my baby,
Lawd, treated dis a-way.

Well, I love my baby,
I tell the worl' I do,
But reason I love her,
Her heart is true.

Gonna lay my head
On some ol' railroad iron,
Das de only way, baby,
To worry you off my min'.

I went to depot,
I looked up on de boa'd,
My baby ain't here,
But she's somewhere on de road.

But I'm goin' to town,
Goin' to ask chief police,
Fo' my baby done quit me
An' I can't have no peace.

An' I'm goin' away, baby,
To worry you off my min',
'Cause you keep me worried
An' bothered all de time.

I wonder whut's de matter,
Lawd, I can't see.
You love some other man, sweet woman,
An' you don't love me.

Befo' I'd stay here
An' let these women mistreat me,
I'd do like a bull frog,
Jump in de deep blue sea.

Wing, however, does not jump into the deep blue sea, although like the other traditional bull frog he does jump from place to place. Concerning the women about whom he sings, he affirmed, "Can't count 'em, take me day after tomorrow to count 'em. Find fifteen or twenty in different cities. New Orleans best place to find most fastest, mo' freer women,—person find gang of 'em in minute.

"But I had some mighty fine women. Fust one was Abbie Jones, 'bout —— Ioway Street. Nex' was in M——, Missouri, Jennie Baker, Susan Baker's daughter. Nex' one St. Louis, lady called Bulah Cotton, Pete Cotton's daughter. Nex' one was in Eas' St. Louis, her name Sylvia Brown. Nex' I had in Poplar Bluff, one dat took my money an' went off, Effie Farlan, had father name George Farlan. Nex' Laura, she's in Memphis, Tennessee, she's 'nother took my money an' gone. Jes' lay down, went to sleep, jes' took money an' gone. Wake up sometimes broke an' hongry, they jes' naturally take my money. Nex' woman was at Columbia, S. C., 'bout las' regular one I had, Mamie Willard, mother an' father dead. Sweethearts I can git plenty of if I got money. If I ain't got none I'se sometimes lonesome, but not always, 'cause sometimes dey feel sorry fer you an' treat you mighty fine anyway."

Wing tells some remarkable stories, evidently products of the perfect technique of appeal and approach, in which formality and easy-going ways are blended with great patience and persistence. This series of adventures alone would make a full sized volume albeit there is no need to publish it abroad. Typical, however, are the chant verses below.

I seed a pretty brown,
Lawd, walkin' down the street,
I sided long up to her,
Said, "Lady, I ain't had nothin' to eat."

Lawd, she don't pay me no min',
Walkin' wid her head hung high.
But still I knows
I'll git dat gal by an' by.

So I walks up behin' her,
And asts her good an' polite,
"Miss, can you tell me
Where po' boy can stay tonight?"

Still she don't pay me no min',
An' she's movin' on her way,
I asks her, "Good Lawd, lady,
Where can po' boy stay?"

I ast her to tell me
If she knows girl name Sady,
'Cause if she does,
I's her man Brady.

Co'se I don't know no Sady
An' I could git place to stay,
But I wants to stay wid dis lady,
So I walks on her way.

So she takes me to her home
An' makes me pallet on de flo';
An' she treats me, baby,
Better 'n I been treated befo'.

Wing says he never stays in any place more than three
weeks, "leastwise never mo' 'n fo'." Sometimes he
walks, sometimes he rides the rods, sometimes when
money is plentiful he rides in the cars. He has had
his tragic and his comic experiences. The spirit of
the road is irrevocably fixed in him and he can think
in no other terms. Some day a Negro artist will
paint him, a Negro story teller will tell his story, a
"high she'ff" will arrest him, a "jedge" will sentence
him, a "cap'n" will "cuss" him, he will "row here few
days longer," then he'll be gone.

CHAPTER XIII

JOHN HENRY: EPIC OF THE
NEGRO WORKINGMAN

LEFT Wing Gordon was and is a very real person, "traveling man" de luxe in the flesh and blood. Not so John Henry, who was most probably a mythical character. Whatever other studies may report, no Negro whom we have questioned in the states of North Carolina, South Carolina and Georgia has ever seen or known of John Henry personally or known any one who has, although it is well understood that he was "mos' fore-handed steel-drivin' man in the world." Still he is none the less real as a vivid picture and example of the good man hero of the race.

Although, like the story of Left Wing, the *John Henry* ballad carries its own intrinsic merit, this song of the black Paul Bunyan of the Negro workingman is significant for other reasons. It is, first of all, a rare creation of considerable originality, dignity and interest. It provides an excellent study in diffusion, and, as soon as the settings, variations, comparisons, and adaptations have been completed, will deserve a special brochure. For the purposes of this volume, however, we shall present simply the *John Henry* ballad in the forms and versions heard within the regions of this collection, with some comparative evidence of the workingman's varied mirror of his hero. John Henry is still growing in reputation and in stature and in favor with the Negro singer, ranging in repute from the ordinary fore-handed steel-driving man to a martyred president of the United States struck down, with the hammer in his hand, by some race assassin. One youth reminiscent of all that he had heard, and minded to make his version complete, set down this:

> When John Henry was on his popper's knee,
> The dress he wore it was red;
> And the las' word he said,
> "I gonna die with the hammer in my hand."

We have found a few Negroes who were not clear in their minds about Booker T. Washington, but we have found none in North Carolina, South Carolina, and Georgia who had not heard something some time about John Henry. In other places, however, in Mississippi and Maryland, for instance, we understand he is not so well known. To trace the story of the ballad to its origin [1] is a difficult task and one awaiting the folk-lorist; but to gather these samples of this sort of nomad ballad is a comparatively easy and always delightful task.

There are many versions of the common story. Some hold that John Henry's "captain" made a large wager with the boss of the steel-driving crew that John Henry could beat the steam drill down, and that John Henry did succeed but died with the last stroke of his hammer. Others claim that the wager was John Henry's own doing and that he never could stand the new-fangled steam contraption. Leastwise he died with the hammer in his hand, some claiming in the mountain drilling stone, others in railroad cuts or tun-

---

[1] Prof. J. H. Cox traces *John Henry* to a real person, John Hardy, a Negro who had a reputation in West Virginia as a steel driver and who was hanged for murder in 1894. We are inclined to believe that *John Henry* was of separate origin and has become mixed with the John Hardy story in West Virginia. We have never found a Negro who knew the song as *John Hardy*, and we have no versions which mention the circumstance of the murder and execution. For Cox's discussion and several versions of *John Hardy*, see his *Folk-Songs of The South*, pp. 175-188; also *Journal of American Folk-Lore*, vol. 32, p. 505 et seq. Bibliographies will be found in these references.

nels of various roads recently under construction. But in all cases the central theme is the same: John Henry, powerful steel-driving man, races with the steam-drill and dies with the hammer in his hand.

Of the fragments or variations of *John Henry* there seems to be no end. One at Columbia, South Carolina, sets the standard of conduct as at par with John Henry and affirms that "If I could hammer like John Henry, I'd bro-by, Lawd, I'd bro-by," which was interpreted to mean the act of passing by the whole procession of steel drivers. An Atlanta version represented John Henry as sitting on his mother's knee, whereupon she "looked in his face an' say, 'John Henry, you'll be the death o' me'." Another fragment from an old timer, self-styled "full-handed musicianer," described John Henry as a steel driver who "always drove the steel" and always "beat the steam drill down," and added that if he could drill like John Henry he would "beat all the steam drills down." While most of the versions limited John Henry to steel driving on mountain or railroad, nevertheless there seems to be a general idea that he took turns at being a railroad man, not in the sense of working on the railroad section gangs but as an engineer, perhaps a skilled one. Part of this is the natural story centering around the logical outcome of a railroad man, and part is corruption of the Casey Jones and other noted engineer songs. One opening stanza has it,

> John Henry was a little boy,
> He was leanin' on his father's knee,
> Say, "That big wheel turnin' on Air Line Road,
> Will sure be death o' me,"

while still others thought the K. C. or Frisco or C. & O. roads would be fatal. In the colloquial story, part of which is given later, John Henry usually told his mother and friends, just as did Jagooze and the other railroad men, about his proprietary powers in the noted railroads across the continent. Then there were the references to his firemen and "riders" and the fear of a wreck. Sometimes, as indicative of the changing form, the singer switches off from the standard *John Henry* lines to some other, like "goin' up Decatur wid hat in my hand, lookin' for woman ain't got no man."

For the most part, however, the versions are rather consistent. The chief differences have to do with minor details. The main story is always the same. We are now presenting a dozen or more versions of the song, beginning with what may be called the purer or more composite versions and ending with versions that have strayed far from the simple story of John Henry. The first is a common Chapel Hill version, but even that is varied almost as often as it is sung by different groups. In this and the other versions, John Henry's wife or woman becomes in turn Delia Ann, Lizzie Ann, Polly Ann, or whatever other Ann may be thought of as representing an attractive person. Sometimes John Henry carried her in the "palm of his hand," as indeed he is also reported to have carried his little son. When a child, John Henry also sat on his father's knee as well as his mother's. Sometimes it was seven-, sometimes nine-, sometimes ten-pound hammer that would be the death of him. Sometimes it was the C. & O. tunnel, sometimes steel, sometimes the hammer which was going to bring him down.

JOHN HENRY [1]

A

John Henry was a steel-drivin' 'man,
Carried his hammer all the time;
'Fore he'd let the steam drill beat him down,
Die wid his hammer in his han',
Die wid his hammer in his han'.

John Henry went to the mountain,
Beat that steam drill down;
Rock was high, po' John was small,
Well, he laid down his hammer an' he died,
Laid down his hammer an' he died.

John Henry was a little babe
Sittin' on his daddy's knee,
Said, "Big high tower on C. & O. road
Gonna be the death o' me,
Gonna be the death o' me."

John Henry had a little girl,
Her name was Polly Ann.
John was on his bed so low,
She drove with his hammer like a man,
Drove with his hammer like a man.

B

John Henry was a little boy
Sittin' on his papa's knee,
Say, "Papa you know I'm boun' to die,
This hammer be the death of me."

John Henry say one day,
"Man ain't nothin' but a man,
Befo' I'll be dogged aroun'
I'll die wid de hammer in my han'."

---

[1] The music of this version is given in Chapter XIV. For the music of
a version of *John Hardy*, see Campbell and Sharp, *English Folk-Songs From
The Southern Appalachians*, p. 87. There is available also a very good phonograph version of *John Henry*.

John Henry said to his captain,
"Man ain't nothin' but a man.
Befo' I work from sun to sun
I'd die wid de hammer in my han'.'"

John Henry was a steel-drivin' man,
Carried hammer all time in his han';
Befo' he let you beat him down
He'd die wid de hammer in his han'.

John Henry had a little girl,
Name was Polly Ann.
John Henry was on his dyin' bed, O Lawd,
She drove with his hammer like a man.

John Henry went up to the mountain
To beat that steel drill down;
But John Henry was so small, rock so high,
Laid down his hammer an' he died.

C

John Henry was a steel-drivin' man.
He drove so steady an' hard;
Well, they put John Henry in head to drive,
He laid down his hammer an' he cried.

Up stepped girl John Henry loved,
She throwed up her hands and flew,
She 'clare to God,
"John Henry, I been true to you."

"O where did you get yo' new shoes from,
O dat dress dat you wear so fine?"
"I got my shoes from a railroad man,
My dress from a driver in de mine."

John Henry had a little wife,
Dress she wore was blue,
An' she declare to God,
"I always been true to you."

John Henry was a little boy
Sittin' on his papa's knee,
He said to his papa, "Drivin' steel
Is gonna be the death of me."

D

John Henry was a coal black man,
Chicken chocolate brown;
"Befo' I let your steamer get me down,
I die wid my hammer in my han', Lawd, Lawd."

John Henry had a pretty little woman,
She rode that Southbound train;
She stopped in a mile of the station up there,
"Let me hear John Henry's hammer ring, Lawd, Lawd."

John Henry sittin' on the left-han' side
An' the steam drill on the right;
The rock it was so large an' John Henry so small,
He laid down his hammer an' he cried, "Lawd, Lawd."

John Henry had a pretty little woman,
Her name was Julie Ann,
She walked through the lan' with a hammer in her han',
Sayin,' "I drive steel like a man, Lawd, Lawd."

John Henry had a little woman,
Her name was Julie Ann;
John Henry took sick on his work one day,
An' Julie Ann drove steel like a man, Lawd, Lawd.

John Henry had a pretty little boy,
Sittin' in de palm of his han';
He hugged an' kissed him an' bid him farewell,
"O son, do the best you can, Lawd, Lawd."

John Henry was a little boy
Sittin' on his papa's knee,
Looked down at a big piece o' steel,
Saying, "Papa, that'll be the death o' me, Lawd, Lawd."

John Henry had a pretty little woman,
The dress she wore was red,
She went down the track an' never did look back,
Sayin', "I'm goin' where John Henry fell dead, Lawd,
    Lawd."

John Henry had a pretty little girl,
The dress she wore was blue,
She followed him to the graveyard sayin,'
"John Henry I've been true to you, Lawd, Lawd."

E

John Henry had a little wife,
Name was Julia Ann;
John Henry got sick on his dyin' bed,
Julia drove steel like a man,
O Lawd, Julia drove steel like a man.

John Henry had a little woman,
The dress she wore was red,
Went down the track, never look back,
"Goin' where my man is dead,
Lawd, goin' where may man is dead."

John Henry was a little boy
Sittin' on his father's knee,
Say, "Ten-pound hammer gonna be the death o' me,
Lawd, gonna be the death o' me."

John Henry went up to the rock,
Carried his hammer in his han,'
Rock was so tall, John Henry was so small,
Laid down his hammer an' he died,
Lawd, laid down his hammer an' he died.

John Henry had a little woman
An' she always dressed in blue,
She went down track, never look back,
Say, "John Henry I'm always true to you,
Lawd, I'm always true to you."

John Henry on the right side,
Steam drill on the lef';
"Befo' I'll let you beat me down
I die wid de hammer in my han',
Lawd, I'd die wid de hammer in my han'.''

"Who gonna shoe yo' pretty little feet, [1]
Who gonna comb yo' bangs?
Who gonna kiss yo' rose-red lips,
Who gonna be yo' man?
Lawd, who gonna be yo' man?''

"Sweet Papa gonna shoe yo' pretty little feet,
Sister gonna comb yo' bangs,
Mama gonna kiss yo' rose-red lips,
John Henry gonna be yo' man,
Lawd, John Henry gonna be yo' man.''

"Where you get them high top shoes,
That dress you wear so fine?"
"Got my shoes from a railroad man,
My dress from a worker in mine,
Lawd, my dress from worker in mine.''

John Henry said to his captain,
"Man is nothin' but a man,
Befo' I let this rock beat me down
I'd die wid de hammer in may han',
Lawd, I'd die wid de hammer in my han'.''

F

John Henry had a little woman,
The dress she wore was red;
She went on down the railroad track,
Say, "Goin' where John Henry fall dead.''

John Henry said to his captain,
"Lawd, a man ain't nothin' but a man,
Befo' I let a man beat me down
I'd die wid de hammer in my han'.''

---

[1] Stanzas of this kind are frequent in *John Henry*. They came originally from the old English ballad, *The Lass of Roch Royal*. See Child, *The English and Scottish Popular Ballads*, No. 76.

John Henry said to his woman,
"Who gonna shoe yo' little feet?
Who gonna kiss yo' rosy cheeks?
Who gonna be yo' man?

"Where you get them high top shoes,
That dress you wear so fine?"
"Got my shoes from a railroad man,
My dress from a man in the mine."

G

John Henry said to his captain,
"Captain, befo' you leave this town,
If you give me another drink of your corn,
I'll beat yo' steel drill down."

Hammer on the right side,
Bucket on the lef',
"Befo' I let you beat me down
I hammer myself to death."

John Henry up on the mountain top,
Say, "Man ain't nothin' but a man,
Befo' I let you beat me down
I'd die wid de hammer in my han'."

John Henry was a little boy,
He set on his mother's knee,
Cryin', "O Lord, nine-pound hammer
Gonna be the death o' me."

H

John Henry had a little wife
An' he carried her in the palm of his han',
He hug an' kiss her an' bid her farewell
An' told her do the bes' she can.

Chorus:

John Henry was a steel-drivin' man,
John Henry was a steel-drivin' man,
John Henry was a steel-drivin' man,
John Henry was a steel-drivin' man.

John Henry was a little boy
Sittin' on his mother's knee,
Say, "Tunnel on C. & O. road
Gonna be the death o' me."

John Henry said to his shaker,[1]
"Shaker, you better pray;
If I make this six-foot jump,
Tomorrow 'll be yo' buryin' day."

John Henry had a little woman,
Name was Polly Ann,
She took a big hammer an' went to the hills,
Polly Ann drive steel like a man.

I

John Henry told his captain,
"Hand me down my time,
I can make more money on Georgia Southern Road
Than I can on old Coast Line."

John Henry told his captain,
"Man ain't nothin' but a man,
Befo' I let you beat me drivin' steel
I'd die wid de hammer in my han'."

John Henry had a little woman,
The dress she wore was red,
Las' word I heard her say,
"Goin' where my man fall dead."

John Henry told his captain,
"Captain, when you go to town,
Bring me back a ten-pound hammer
So I can drive this steel on down."

J

John Henry told his captain,
"A man ain't nothin' but a man,
Befo' I work from sun to sun
I'd die wid de hammer in my han'."

---

[1] The "shaker" is the man who holds the drill upright and turns it between the strokes of the hammer.

John Henry had a little woman,
Dress she wore was red;
Goin' down railroad weepin' and cryin',
Goin' where John Henry fall dead.

Say, I ain't gonna work much longer,
Ain't gonna work on no farm;
An' I'm gonna stay here till pay-day,
Ain't gonna do nobody no harm.

"Where'd you git them pretty little shoes?
Where'd you git that dress so fine?"
"Got my shoes from a railroad man,
Dress from a man in the mine."

"Who's gonna shoe yo' pretty little feet?
Who's gonna comb yo' bangs?
Who's gonna kiss yo' rosy cheeks?
Who's gonna be yo' man?

"Papa gonna shoe yo' pretty little feet,
Sister gonna comb yo' bangs;
Mama gonna kiss yo' rosy cheeks,
John Henry gonna be yo' man."

John Henry had a little woman,
Name was Polly Ann;
John Henry got sick an' couldn't hit a lick,
Polly Ann hit steel like a man.

John Henry told his captain,
"Captain, when you go to town,
Oh, bring me back a nine-pound hammer
So I can drive this steel on down."

John Henry was a little boy
Settin' on his papa's knee,
Say, "The tunnel on the L. & N.
Gonna be the death o' po' me."

John Henry had a little girl,
Name was Nellie Ann;
John Henry took sick an' had to go home,
Every day po' Nellie drove steel like a man.

John Henry had a little pistol,
He carried it around in his han'
Well, look way over in Southwest,
You will find a steel-drivin' man.

"Who gonna buy yo' pretty little shoes?
Who gonna be yo' man?
Who gonna buy yo' dress so fine?
While I'm in some distant lan'?"

John Henry bought a pistol,
Put it up in forty-fo' frame,
He look over in Southwest,
Spied that steel-drivin' man.

John Henry's wife settin' on do'-step cryin',
Say, "Where po' John Henry gone?"
John Henry's wife settin' on do'-step cryin',
Say, "Where po' John Henry gone?"

John Henry's wife said to his chillun,
"Little chillun, don't you worry none,
'Cause mama goin' down to steel-drivin' place
Where po' daddy done gone."

Children come runnin' and cryin',
"Mama, what we gonna do?
News done reach gran'ma's do',
Papa done fall stone dead."

People went up in the mountain,
Say mountain was fallin' in.
John Henry say it was sad mistake,
"Nothin' but my hammer in the win'."

John Henry say to his captain,
"Man ain't nothin' but a man,
Oh, befo' I let steel drill beat me down
I die wid de hammer in my han'."

John Henry say to his captain,
"I have been with you ninety-nine-years,
An', captain, you don't hurry nobody,
But always hurry me."

K

John Henry was a little boy,
Was settin' 'roun' playin' in the san',
Two young ladies come a-ridin' by,
Say, "I want you to be my man."

John Henry was a little boy,
Settin' on his mamy's knee,
Say, "Dat ol' nine-poun' hammer
Gonna be the death o' me."

John Henry was a cruel boy,
Never did look down;
But when he start to drivin' steel
He ever-mo' did drive it down.

John Henry went to cap'n Monday
All worried in his min',
Say, "Give me a heavy axe,
Let me tear dis ol' mountain down."

John Henry told the captain,
"Cap'n, when you go to town,
Bring me back a ten-poun' hammer
An' I lay dis ol' sev'n-poun' down."

John Henry went to captain,
"What mo' you want me to have?
Say, han' me drink o' ol' white gin,
An' I'll be a steel-drivin' man."

John Henry had a little woman,
The dress she wore was red,
She went down de track, never look back,
Say, "I goin' where my man fall dead."

"Who gonna shoe my pretty little feet?
Mommer gonna glove my han'.
Popper gonna kiss my rosy cheeks,
John Henry gonna be my man."

John Henry went to captain,
Say, "Man ain't nothin' but a man.
Befo' I let you beat me down
I die wid de hammer in my han'."

John Henry had a little woman,
Name was Lizzie Ann.
Say she got her dress from man in mine
An' her shoes from railroad man.

John Henry on right,
Steam drill on lef',
"Befo' I let steam drill beat me down
I'll drive my fool self to death.

"I drill all time,
I drill all day,
I drill all way from Rome
To Decatur in one day."

John Henry say,
"Tell my mother
If she want to see me,
Buy ticket all way to Frisco."

John Henry on way to Frisco,
Wid orders in his han',
Say, "All you rounders who want to flirt,
Here come a woman wid a hobble-skirt."

John Henry say to his captain
Befo' he lef' town,
"If you give me 'nother drink o' yo' co'n,
I'll beat yo' steel drill down."

It would take a large volume to record all of the ways
in which John Henry is known to the Negro worker
and singer. He is known far and wide in song and
story and he is the hero of hundreds of thousands of
black toilers. Negroes who do work that requires
rhythmic movements, such as digging or driving steel,
naturally like to dwell upon the thought of the great

John Henry, and they make work songs about the great hero. The four songs which follow are not only good examples of this kind of work song, but reveal something of the worker's feeling for John Henry.

Dis Here Hammer Kill John Henry

Dis here hammer, hammer
Kill John Henry,
Kill John Henry;
Dis here hammer, hammer
Kill John Henry,
Can't kill me,
O Lawd, can't kill me.

If I Could Hammer Like John Henry

If I could hammer like John Henry,
If I could hammer like John Henry,
Lawd, I'd be a man,
Lawd, I'd be a man.

If I could hammer like John Henry,
If I could hammer like John Henry,
I'd bro-by, Lawd,
I'd bro-by.

Nine-poun' hammer kill John Henry,
Nine-poun' hammer kill John Henry,
Won't kill me,
Lawd, won't kill me.

I been hammerin',
All 'roun' mountain,
Won't kill me, babe,
Lawd, won't kill me.

Heard Mighty Rumblin'

Heard mighty rumblin',
Heard mighty rumblin',
Heard mighty rumblin'
Under the groun'.

Well, heard mighty rumblin',
Under the groun',
Under the groun',
Mus' be John Henry turnin' aroun'.

Up on the mountain,
Up on the mountain,
Well, up on the mountain,
Heard John Henry cryin'.

Heard John Henry cryin',
Heard John Henry cryin',
Well, I heard John Henry cryin',
"An' I won't come down."

JOHN HENRY WAS A MAN O' MIGHT

John Henry was a man o' might,
John Henry was a man o' might,
John Henry was a man o' might,
He beat de iron man down.

John Henry had a hammer han,'[1]
An' he beat de iron man down.

"Lawd, Lawd, boss," he cried,
"De iron man too much fo' me."

An' dey laid John Henry low,
He won't swing dat hammer no mo'.

John Henry was big an' strong
But de iron man brung 'im down.

John Henry was big an' brown
But de iron man brung him down.

John Henry say, "I got to go,
I can't swing de ball no mo'."

John Henry was a mighty man,
An' he swing dat hammer.

---

[1] The first line of each stanza is sung three times as indicated in the first stanza.

In story John Henry's deeds often assume magnificent proportions. Indeed, the stories about him are in many respects more interesting than the songs, for the stories usually have more range and reflect more imagination than the songs. Occasionally one can find a Negro who will tell the story simply and without exaggeration, but one usually gets a version which is more or less embellished with the legendary attributes and attainments of John Henry. In the following story, John Henry is credited with such powers as would make him a close rival of Paul Bunyan himself. [1]

"One day John Henry lef' rock quarry on way to camp an' had to go through woods an' fiel'. Well, he met big black bear an' didn't do nothin' but shoot 'im wid his bow an' arrer, an' arrer went clean through bear an' stuck in big tree on other side. So John Henry pulls arrer out of tree an' pull so hard he falls back 'gainst 'nother tree which is full o' flitterjacks, an' first tree is full o' honey, an' in pullin' arrer out o' one he shaken down honey, an' in fallin' 'gainst other he shaken down flitterjacks. Well, John Henry set there an' et honey an' flitterjacks an' set there an' et honey an' flitterjacks, an' after while when he went to git up to go, button pop off'n his pants an' kill a rabbit mo' 'n hundred ya'ds on other side o' de tree. An' so up jumped brown baked pig wid sack o' biscuits on his back, an' John Henry et him too.

"So John Henry gits up to go on through woods to camp for supper, 'cause he 'bout to be late an' he mighty hongry for his supper. John Henry sees lake down hill and thinks he'll git him a drink o' water, cause he's thirsty, too, after eatin' honey an' flitterjacks an'

---

[1] This story was recorded at Chapel Hill, N. C., but, as far as we can tell it came originally from Stone Mountain, Ga. It is given as nearly as possible in the words in which it was told.

brown roast pig an' biscuits, still he's hongry yet.
An' so he goes down to git drink water an' finds lake
ain't nothin' but lake o' honey, an' out in middle
dat lake ain't nothin but tree full o' biscuits. An' so
John Henry don't do nothin' but drink dat lake o'
honey dry. An' he et the tree full o' biscuits, too.
"An' so 'bout that time it begin' to git dark, an' John
Henry sees light on hill an' he think maybe he can git
sumpin to eat, cause he's mighty hongry after big day
drillin'. So he look 'roun' an' see light on hill an'
runs up to house where light is an' ast people livin'
dere, why'n hell dey don't give him sumpin' to eat,
'cause he ain't had much. An' so he et dat, too.

"Gee-hee, hee, dat nigger could eat! But dat ain't
all, cap'n. Dat nigger could wuk mo' 'n he could eat.
He's greates' steel driller ever live, regular giaunt, he
wus; could drill wid his hammer mo' 'n two steam
drills, an' some say mo' 'n ten. Always beggin' boss
to git 'im bigger hammer, always beggin' boss git 'im
bigger hammer. John Henry wus cut out fer big
giaunt driller. One day when he wus jes' few weeks
ol' settin' on his mammy's knee he commence cryin'
an' his mommer say, "John Henry, whut's matter,
little son?" An' he up an' say right den an' dere dat
nine-poun' hammer be death o' him. An' so sho'
'nough he grow up right 'way into bigges' steel driller
worl' ever see. Why dis I's tellin' you now wus jes'
when he's young fellow; waits til' I tells you 'bout his
drillin' in mountains an' in Pennsylvania. An' so one
day he drill all way from Rome, Georgia, to D'catur,
mo' 'n a hundred miles drillin' in one day, an' I ain't
sure dat wus his bes' day. No, I ain't sure dat wus his
bes' day.

"But, boss, John Henry wus a regular boy, not lak
some o' dese giaunts you read 'bout not likin' wimmin

an' nothin'. John Henry love to come to town same
as any other nigger, only mo' so. Co'se he's mo'
important an' all dat, an' co'se he had mo' wimmin
'an anybody else, some say mo' 'n ten, but as to dat I
don't know. I means, boss, mo' wimmen 'an ten men,
'cause, Lawd, I specs he had mo' 'n thousand wimmin'.
An' John Henry wus a great co'tin' man, too, cap'n.
Always wus dat way. Why, one day when he settin'
by his pa' in san' out in front o' de house, jes' few weeks
old, women come along and claim him fer deir man.
An' dat's funny, too, but it sho' wus dat way all his
life. An' so when he come to die John Henry had mo'
wimmin, all dressed in red an' blue an' all dem fine
colors come to see him dead, if it las' thing they do,
an' wus mighty sad sight, people all standin' 'roun',
both cullud an' white."

Of course, no Negro believes that the foregoing story
is true. But there are innumerable stories which stay
within the bounds of possibility—though not always
probability, to be sure—and which are thoroughly
believed by the Negroes who tell them. One of the
most widespread of these, and at the same time interesting and artistic, was concluded as follows by a
North Carolina Negro workman:

"An' John Henry beat dat ol' steam drill down, but
jes' as he took his las' stroke he fell over daid wid de
hammer in his han'. Dey buried him dere in de
tunnel, an' now dey got his statue carved in solid rock
at de mouth o' de Big Ben' tunnel on de C. & O.—das
right over dere close to Asheville somewhere. No,
I ain't never been dere, but dere he stan', carved in
great big solid rock wid de hammer in his han'.

CHAPTER XIV

SOME TYPICAL NEGRO TUNES

WE have pointed out again and again the utter futility of trying to describe accurately the singing of a group of Negroes when they are at their best. A group of twenty workers singing, carrying various parts, suiting song to work, and vying with one another for supremacy in variations and innovations—this is a scene which defies musical notation and description. And yet the picture which we have tried to present in this volume would certainly be incomplete without the addition of some of the simple melodies of typical workaday songs. They are added, therefore, merely as final touches to the picture rather than as attempts to reproduce the complex harmonies of Negro songs.

Heretofore the spirituals have received most of the attention of those who were working toward the preservation of Negro music. The secular songs have nothing like the standardization of words and music that the spirituals have, simply because they have not been preserved. It is inevitable, however, that due attention will be given to Negro secular music. Indeed much has recently been done toward that end. [1] But the task of recording the majority of Negro secular tunes is yet to be done. It is to be hoped that the forthcoming volume of secular songs which is being edited by James Weldon Johnson will go a long way toward giving the Negro's secular music the place which it deserves.

---

[1] For a discussion of the recent collections of Negro songs, see Guy B. Johnson, "Some Recent Contributions to the Study of American Negro Songs," *Social Forces*, June, 1926.

Any one who has tried to record the music of Negro songs knows that it is very difficult to do more than approximate the tunes as they are actually sung. Several reasons may be cited to account for this. In the first place, there are slurs and minute gradations in pitch in Negro songs which it is impossible to represent in ordinary musical notation. Some of these effects can be reproduced on a stringed instrument, but they cannot be shown on a musical scale which is only divided into half-step changes of pitch. A notation in the form of curved lines would come nearer representing the Negro's singing than does the system of definite notes along a staff. It is what the Negro sings between the lines and spaces that makes his music so difficult to record.

Another factor which must be reckoned with is the inconsistency of the singer. When the recorder thinks that he has finally succeeded in getting a phrase down correctly and asks the singer to repeat it "just one more time," he often finds that the response is quite different from any previous rendition. Requests for further repetition may bring out still other variations or a return to the previous version. Again, after the notation has been made from the singing of the first stanza of a song, the collector may be chagrined to find that none of the other stanzas is sung to exactly the same tune. The variations are not marked. They are elusive and teasing, and they add beauty to the song.

How often the song collector wishes for some instrument which will record group singing in its native haunts! He cannot hope to catch by ear alone all of the parts—and there are undoubtedly six or eight of many of these songs—that go into the making of those rare harmonies which only a group of Negro workers

can produce. If he coaxes the singers to keep re-
peating their song, some of them become self-conscious
and drop out. Perhaps the whole group will refuse
to sing any more. If perchance he gets one or two
singers to give him some special help, he gets but a
suggestion of the group effect. He must be contented
with securing the leading part of the song and harmo-
nizing it later as best he can.

So these rare work harmonies have never been faithfully reproduced in musical notation. [1] Rather than
give an artificial harmonization to the tunes recorded
in this chapter, we are presenting only the leading part
of each song.

Since several of the songs in this chapter are work
songs, let us examine for a moment the technique of the
worker-singer. Many work songs, of course, are not
really work songs except in the sense that they are sung
during work. When the work is such that it does not
necessitate continuous rhythmic movements, one song
is about as good as another. But rhythmic movements, being especially adapted to song accompaniment, have given rise to a distinct type of work song.
Digging, hammering, steel-driving, rowing, and many
other kinds of work fall in the rhythmic class. The
technique for all of these is practically the same.

Let us take digging as an example, since it is a very
common type of Negro labor in the South. Typical
pick-song patterns are as follows:

> I got a rainbow,
> Rainbow 'roun' my shoulder;
> I got a rainbow,
> Rainbow 'roun' my shoulder;
> 'Tain't gonna rain,
> Lawd, Lawd, 'tain't gonna rain.

---

[1] The nearest approach ever made to accurate recording of such songs
is found in the work of the late Natalie Curtis Burlin. See her *Negro Folk
Songs*, Hampton Series, vols. III and IV.

Well, she asked me
In her parlor
An' she cooled me
Wid her fan;
Lawd, she whispered
To her mother,
"Mama, I love
That dark-eyed man."

Now in the type of song illustrated by the first of the
above patterns the strokes of the pick are not all of
equal length. The rhythm of the song demands a
short stroke alternated with a longer stroke. In the
second type of song, however, the meter is such that
all of the strokes of the pick may be of equal length.
At the end of each line there is a cæsura or pause.
This represents the time during which the worker
swings his pick from the upright position to the ground.
When the pick strikes the ground, the worker gives a
grunt, loosens the pick, and raises it. It is during
this loosening and upward movement that he sings.
The down-stroke calls for much more effort than
raising the pick, so he rarely ever sings on the down-
stroke. The time required for a digging stroke is,
however, shorter than the time required for loosening
and raising the pick, so that ordinarily the pauses in
the song are relatively brief.

It is in a group that the work song is to be heard at
its best. When a group is digging and singing, picks
are swung in unison. On a few occasions we have
observed that one or two men took their strokes out
of unison in order to sing certain exclamations or
echoes during the pauses in the singing of their companions. This, however, is a rare procedure, for the
most striking variations in both music and words can
be introduced without breaking the unison of the
strokes.

To call a song a pick song does not mean that it is not also a good song for general purposes. *I Got a Rainbow, I Don't Want No Trouble Wid de Walker,* and other pick songs are quite effective when sung as solos with guitar accompaniment. On the other hand, many general songs can easily be converted into pick songs by slight changes in meter. [1]

A few of the tunes presented in the following pages are the older Negro secular tunes. *Stagolee* and *Railroad Bill* are rarely heard now, but they were common twenty years ago, and their music is included in the present collection for whatever its preservation may be worth. The words of *Stagolee, Railroad Bill* and *She Asked Me in de Parlor* are reprinted in full from *The Negro and His Songs,* but only the first stanzas of the other songs are given, since the rest of the words can be found in the preceding chapters of the present volume. The songs in every case are written in the key in which they were sung.

STAGOLEE

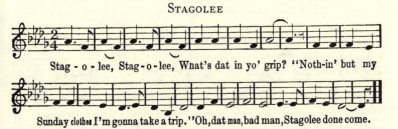

Stag - o - lee, Stag - o - lee, What's dat in yo' grip? "Noth-in' but my Sunday clothes I'm gonna take a trip."Oh,dat man,bad man,Stagolee done come.

Stagolee, Stagolee, what's dat in yo' grip?
Nothin' but my Sunday clothes, I'm gonna to take a trip,
Oh, dat man, bad man, Stagolee done come.

---

[1] For other discussions of work songs, see Natalie Curtis Burlin, *Negro Folk Songs,* vols. III and IV; Dorothy Scarborough, *On the Trail of Negro Folk Songs,* chapter VIII; R. Emmet Kennedy, *Mellows;* Odum and Johnson, *The Negro and His Songs,* chapter VIII.

Stagolee, Stagolee, where you been so long?
I been out on de battle fiel' shootin' an' havin' fun.
Oh, dat man, *etc*.

Stagolee was a bully man, an' ev'ybody knowed
When dey seed Stagolee comin' to give Stagolee de road.

Stagolee started out, he give his wife his han';
"Goodby, darlin', I'm goin' to kill a man."

Stagolee killed a man an' laid him on de flo',
What's dat he kill him wid?   Dat same ol' fohty-fo'.

Stagolee killed man an' laid him on his side,
What's dat he kill him wid?   Dat same ol' fohty-five.

Out of house an' down de street Stagolee did run,
In his hand he held a great big smok'n' gun.

Stagolee, Stagolee, I'll tell you what I'll do;
If you'll git me out'n dis trouble I'll do as much for you.

Ain't it a pity, ain't it a shame?
Stagolee was shot, but he don't want no name.

Stagolee, Stagolee, look what you done done:
Killed de best ol' citerzen, now you'll have to be hung.

Stagolee cried to de jury, "Please don't take my life,
I have only three little children an' one little lovin' wife."

Railroad Bill

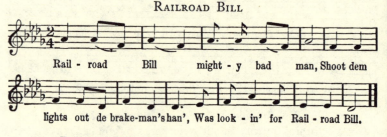

Rail - road   Bill   might - y   bad   man, Shoot dem
lights out de brake-man's han', Was look - in' for Rail - road Bill.

Railroad Bill mighty bad man,
Shoot dem lights out o' de brakeman's han',
        Was lookin' fer Railroad Bill.

Railroad Bill mighty bad man,
Shoot the lamps all off de stan',
    An' it's lookin' fer Railroad Bill.

First on table, next on wall;
Ol' corn whiskey cause of it all,
    It's lookin' fer Railroad Bill.

Ol' McMillan had a special train;
When he got there was shower of rain,
    Wus lookin' fer Railroad Bill.

Ev'ybody tol' him he better turn back;
Railroad Bill wus goin' down track,
    An' it's lookin' fer Railroad Bill.

Well, the policemen all dressed in blue,
Comin' down sidewalk two by two,
    Wus lookin' fer Railroad Bill.

Railroad Bill had no wife,
Always lookin' fer somebody's life,
    An' it's lookin' fer Railroad Bill.

Railroad Bill was the worst ol' coon:
Killed McMillan by de light o' de moon,
    It's lookin' fer Railroad Bill.

Ol' Culpepper went up on number five,
Goin' bring him back, dead or alive,
    Wus lookin' fer Railroad Bill.

She Asked Me in de Parlor

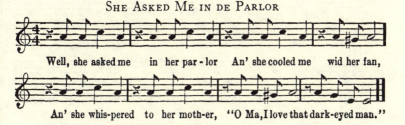

Well, she asked me in her par - lor An' she cooled me wid her fan,
An' she whis-pered to her moth-er, "O Ma, I love that dark-eyed man."

Well, she ask me in her parlor
An' she cooled me wid her fan,
An' she whispered to her mother,
"Mama, I love that dark-eyed man."

Well, I ask her mother for her
An' she said she was too young.
Lawd, I wished I never had seen her
An' I wished she'd never been born.

Well, I led her to de altar,
An' de preacher give his comman',
An' she swore by God that made her
That she never love another man.

John Henry

John Hen - ry was a steel-driv-in' man, Ca'd his hammer all the 'time,........ An' be - fo' he'd let the steam-drill beat him down, Die with the hammer in his han', Die with the hammer in his han'.

Goin' Down That Lonesome Road

Goin' down that lone-some road, Oh, goin' down that lone - some road, An' I won't be treat-ed this - a way. Springs on my bed done brok - en down, An' I ain't got no-where to lay my head.

Reason I Stay on de Job So Long

Reason I stay on de job so long, Gimme flam-donies an' de cof-fee strong.

TOL' MY CAP'N THAT MY FEET WAS COL'

Tol' my cap'n that my feet was col', "God damn yo' feet, let the car wheel roll."

SHOOT THAT BUFFALO

Went down to Raleigh, Was nev-er there be-fo', White folks on de feather bed,

Nig-gers on de flo'. Shoot dat buf-fa, shoot dat lo, Shoot dat buf-fa-lo.

I GOT A RAINBOW

A

Oh, ev-'ry-where I, where I look this morn-in', It looks like

rain, Lawd, O my Lawd, looks like rain, it looks like rain, Lawd, O my Lawd,

looks like rain, Oh, ev-'ry-where I, where I look this morn-in'.

I GOT A RAINBOW

B

Oh, ev-'ry-where I, Where I look dis morn-in', Oh, ev-'ry-where I,

Where I look dis morn-in', It look like rain, Lawd, Lawd, looks like rain.

I Don't Want No Trouble Wid de Walker

Oh, I don't want no, Want no trouble wid de walk-er; Oh, I don't want no,

Want no trouble wid de walker. Wanta go home, Lawd, Lawd, wanta go home.

If I'd Known My Cap'n Was Blin'

If I'd a-known my cap'n was blin', dar-lin',

If I'd a-known my cap'n was blin', dar-lin', If I'd a-known my

cap'n was blin', I wouldn'-a went to work till half-pas' nine, dar-lin'.

I Got a Muley

I got a mul-ey, Mul-ey on the mountain, call him Jer-ry; Oh, I can

ride him, Ride him an-y time I wanta, All day long, Lawd. Lawd, all day long.

SHOT MY PISTOL IN THE HEART OF TOWN

O - o - o - h, L - a - a - w - d, Shot my pis - tol

in de heart o-town,......... Lawd, de big Chief holled, "Don't you blow me down.

CHAPTER XV

TYPES OF PHONO-PHOTOGRAPHIC
RECORDS OF NEGRO SINGERS

WE have referred often in these pages to the wealth of material found in the great variety and number of the Negro's songs. We have appraised the collections which have been published and those which are to come as valuable source material for the study of folk life and art and especially for their value in the portrayal of representative Negro life. Adequate analysis and presentation of these values will be possible only after a number of the other collections have been completed and comprehensive studies made.

There are other values not yet presented. For example, the scientific study of the Negro's musical ability has barely begun, but it promises much. The work of Professor Carl E. Seashore and others has resulted in the formulation of various tests and methods for studying musical talent and singing ability. Many valuable studies have been reported from various psychological laboratories. One of the latest developments in this field is the phono-photographic method of recording voices. In this method the phono-photographic machine makes it possible to take pictures of sound waves of all kinds. Among other things, it registers the most delicate variations in pitch, variations which are often too subtle for the human ear to perceive. In short, it gives a picture of exactly what a voice or a musical instrument does.

Naturally this method of sound wave analysis may be of untold value in the study of the human voice. It enables the singer to see his voice in detail. It furnishes the scientist with data for the study of the qualities which make a voice good or poor. It opens up many possibilities, both practical and theoretical, as a method of voice analysis.

Of special interest and importance is the application of this method to the study of Negro singers and Negro voices. It was therefore a fortunate turn of circumstances which made it possible for the authors of this volume to join Professor Seashore and Dr. Milton Metfessel of the University of Iowa in making extensive phono-photographic studies of various Negro singers during the fall of 1925, with headquarters at the University of North Carolina Institute for Research in Social Science. Professor Seashore was able to coöperate personally in the work at Hampton, while Dr. Metfessel remained throughout the entire period of the study. [1]

Among the types of Negro singers whose voices were subjected to the phono-photographic process were practically all of the common types which we have been recording in the pages of this volume and of *The Negro and His Songs*. There were the typical laborers, working with pick and shovel. There was the lonely singer, with his morning yodel or "holler." There were the skilled workers with voices more or less trained by practice and formal singing. There was the more nearly primitive type, swaying body and limb with singing. The noted quartet from Hampton Institute, as well as individual singers there, coöperated. Men and women from the North Carolina College for Negroes represented other types. Quartets

---

[1] Dr. Metfessel, using the perfected machine which long years of work at the University of Iowa psychological laboratories have produced, was successful in obtaining a large number of satisfactory records. He also took moving pictures of the singers. Needless to say, we are indebted to him for the material of this chapter.

and individuals from the high schools at Chapel Hill
and Raleigh, North Carolina, were still other types.
Finally the voices of one hundred and fifty Negro
children from the Orange County Training School at
Chapel Hill and the Washington School at Raleigh
were recorded. Types of songs included in the ex-
periments were the gang work song, the pick-and-
shovel song and various other work songs, the yodel,
the "1926 model laugh," the blues, formal quartet
music, spirituals, and children's songs. It would thus
appear that both the selections and the numbers were
adequate to make a valuable beginning in a new phase
of the subject.

The results of this study will be published fully later.
The present chapter is in no sense a report of the
results. It is intended merely to describe the phono-
photographic study, to give some examples of records
obtained during the study, and to indicate certain
possibilities of this method as a scientific means of
research into Negro singing abilities and qualities.

The following explanation will suffice to acquaint
the reader with the method of reading the photographic
records presented in this chapter. Along the left side
of each graph are the notes of the scale in half steps.
When the heavy line which represents the voice rises
or falls one space on the graph, the voice has changed a
half tone in pitch. Time value is shown along the bottom of the graph. The vertical bars occurring every
5.55 spaces along the bottom mark off intervals of one
second.

If one were to sing a perfectly rigid tone, its photographic record would be a horizontal straight line.
Such a thing is very rare, however, in any type of
singing, for most sustained tones photograph as more
or less irregular wavy lines. Indeed, a voice whose
sustained tones photographed as a straight line would

not produce as good tones as one with rapid and regular variations of the vocal cords. A good singing voice possesses what is called the *vibrato*. In terms of the photographic records, the pitch vibrato consists of a rise and fall of pitch of about half a tone about six times a second. In Figure I are given samples of tones photographed by Seashore and Metfessel from the singing of *Annie Laurie* by Lowell Welles. The first represents the singing of the word "dew" in the line, "Where early fa's the dew." The second is the word "and" from the line, "And for bonnie Annie Laurie." The vibrato is present in both tones. Note how the voice line varies above or below the note E on "dew" and F-sharp on "and," sometimes as much as a quarter of a tone. Note also the smoothness and regularity of the pitch fluctuations. It is this smoothness of the vibrato which characterizes good singing.

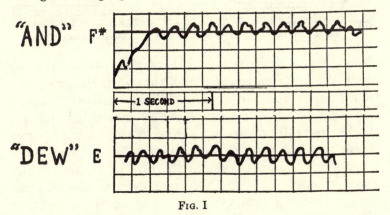

FIG. I

To illustrate their scope, methods, and possibilities three specimens of photographic records of Negro voices are presented: a song, *I Got a Muley*,[1] by

[1]The tune is slightly different from the music of the song of the same name given in Chapter XIV. It is variously called *I Got a Mule on the Mountain*, *I Got Mule Named Jerry*, *I Got a Muley*, *Jerry on Mountain*.

Odell Walker; a yodel or "holler," as it is commonly called, by Cleve Atwater; and Cleve's "1926 Model Laugh."

Figure II is the photographic notation of *I Got a Muley*. The music of the song as best it can be represented in ordinary notation is given below. Several interesting things are revealed by the song picture in Figure II. [1] For one thing, we have here a picture of some of those elusive slurs which are so common among Negro singers. Take the words "muley on a mount'n" in Figure II-A, for example.

I GOT A MULEY,   MULEY ON A MOUNT'N CALL 'IM JERRY;   I GOT A   MULEY,

MULEY ON A MOUNT'N CALL'IM JERRY.   I CAN RIDE HIM,   RIDE'IM ANY   TIME   I

WAN' UH;   I CAN   RIDE   HIM   RIDE'IM ANY   TIME   I   WAN'UH, LAWD, LAWD, ALL DAY LONG.

When one hears these words as they were sung by Odell Walker, one is apt to feel that with the exception of the last syllable of "mount'n" they are all sung on the same pitch. The graph shows that this is not so. There are really drops in pitch of one and a half or two whole tones at two places in this phrase. Or take the word "ride," as it occurs in the phrase, "ride 'im any time I wan' uh," which phrase occurs twice in the song. One can tell while listening to the song that there is some sort of slur present, but it is impossible to tell by means of the ear alone exactly what is happening. The graph reveals the fact that the singer

---

[1] A measure on the graph is equivalent to approximately nine spaces on the horizontal scale. Note that the singer did not keep accurate time. His measures range from six to twelve spaces.

actually begins the word "ride" between D-sharp and E and carries it as high as G-sharp. The outstanding tone heard, however, is G-sharp. Other pitch changes not shown in the ordinary musical notation may be easily detected by the reader.

The vibrato is present in places in the record of this song. It section A there is a trace of it on the word "muley" the first time it occurs. In section B there is an approach to it on the word "Jerry." In section C it occurs on the word "ride" the first time it appears. In section D there is a tendency toward it on "Lawd, Lawd," but is shows best in "long", the last word of the song. A comparison with the examples of artistic singing in Figure I shows that our Negro workman's vibrato is rough and irregular and that it does not maintain a steady general pitch level as does Welles's vibrato. It must be borne in mind, however, that this particular song does not afford good opportunties for sustained tones and that the Negro singer's vibrato might have shown to better advatnage on a different song.

In Figure III is a picture of a yodel or "holler." It is the sort of thing which one hears from field hands as they go to work in the morning, or from some gay-spirited pick-and-shovel man as he begins digging on a frosty morning.

No attempt is made to include the ordinary musical notation of the yodel, for it would give but a suggestion of the vocal idiosyncrasies involved in the execution of the yodel. The most remarkable thing about this record is the sudden changes of pitch which it portrays. In Figure III-A just at the beginning of the fifth second interval the voice takes a sudden drop. Then it rises from F to G in the octave above in about a third of a second. In section B of the yodel, near the end of the fifth second interval, the same spectacular rise

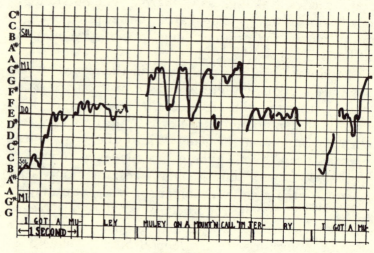

Fig. II-A

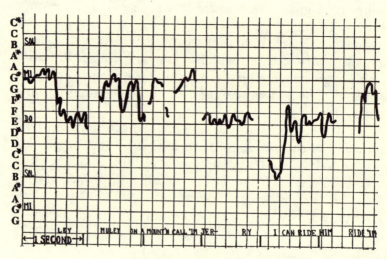

Fig. II-B

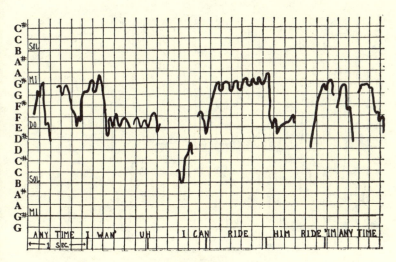

Fig. II-C

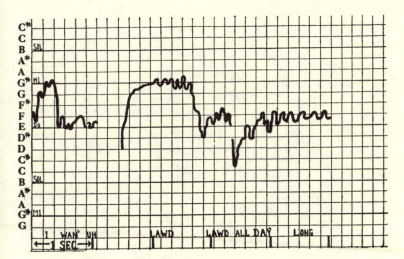

Fig. II-D

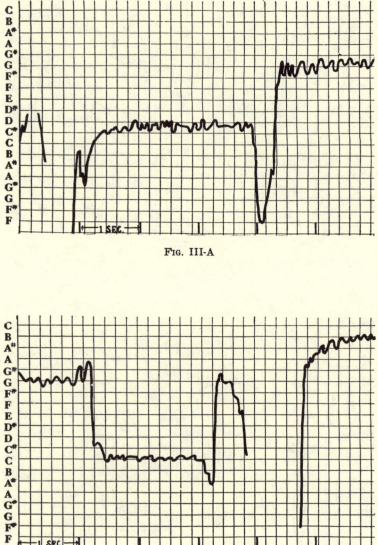

FIG. III-A

FIG. III-B

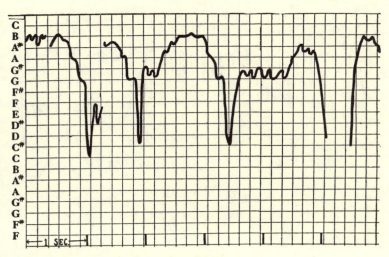

FIG. III-C

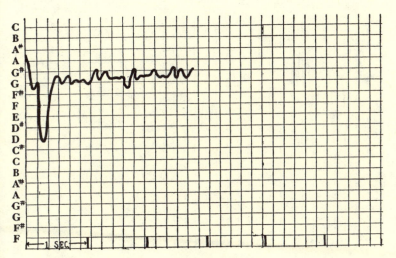

FIG. III-D

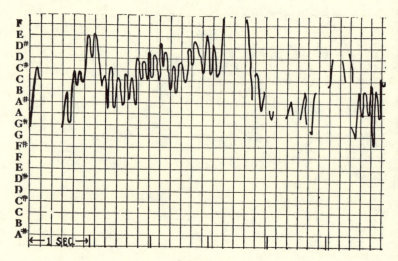

FIG. IV-A

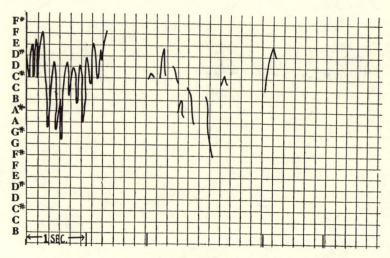

FIG. IV-B

occurs, this time from F-sharp to G-sharp in about one-tenth of a second. Still more remarkable are the several rapid rises and falls in pitch in section C. In the production of such sudden changes the vocal cords must undergo a snap. Even in speech, where pitch changes are very rapid, such sudden ascents and descents do not occur.

It is also interesting to note that the vibrato is present at times in the yodel. It is fairly plain on C-sharp along the middle of section A and still better on G at the end of the same section. It also shows at the end of section B, continuing into section C; and the yodel ends with a semi-vibrato. There is an approach to it in several other places. The vibrato of our Negro worker, however, is rather erratic and wavering in comparison with the vibrato of the vocal artist in Figure I. Yet one must remember that our subjects, both in Figure II and Figure III, were Negro workers whose voices have never had a touch of formal training.

In Figure IV we have a photographic record of a hearty Negro laugh. Its musical quality is at once evident. In the first three seconds of the laugh there is an unusual effect. It would not be called a vibrato because the pitch changes are too rapid and too extensive to give the vibrato effect. Near the beginning of the fifth second of the laugh the voice breaks up into a series of interrupted speech sounds. During the sixth second it suddenly becomes musical again and remains so for about two seconds. Then, after a rest, (see section B) the speech sounds reappear and continue intermittently to the end of the laugh.

These observations indicate some of the possibilities of the phono-photographic method of studying Negro voices and Negro songs. When the complete results of the recent study are ready for publication we may have data which will make it possible to compare scientifically the voices of different kinds of Negro singers as well as the voices of Negro and white singers.

Other studies and correlations may be made through the articulation of the moving pictures of the singers, their faces, their bodily movements, their emotional expressions, and whatever reactions the camera may reveal. In nearly all instances where phono-photographic records were made of Negro voices in the recent study, moving pictures were made of the singers. In addition to these, moving pictures were made of groups of workmen while singing. Some remarkable examples of skill in movement, of coördination of song with 'work, of mixture of humor, pathos, and recklessness with work and song were brought to light. These have been incorporated into a series of three reels. Some of these pictures of facial expression during singing will be included in the report of the study when it is published in complete form.

Many interesting questions may find their solutions if the scientific method is applied to the study of Negro singing ability. Is the vibrato a native endowment? Is the vibrato more frequent among Negroes than among whites? At what age does it appear in the voice?[1] What other qualities cause the rank and file of Negroes to excel as singers? Is the Negro's capacity for harmony greater than the white man's? Is his sense of rhythm better? These are some of the questions which science should be able to answer in the near future.

---

[1] A study of the voices of white and Negro school children now being made by Milton Metfessel and Guy B. Johnson may throw some light upon some of these questions.

SELECTED BIBLIOGRAPHY [1]

BOOKS

ABBOT, F. H., and SWAN, A. J., *Eight Negro Songs.* Enoch & Sons, New York, 1923. Eight songs from Bedford County, Virginia. Explanatory comments and notes on dialect are given for each song.

ALLEN, W. F., and others, *Slave Songs of the United States.* New York, 1867. Words and music of 136 songs are given.

ARMSTRONG, M. F., *Hampton and Its Students.* New York, 1874. Fifty plantation songs.

BALLANTA, N. G. J., *St. Helena Island Spirituals.* G. Schirmer, New York, 1925. A collection of 115 spirituals from Penn School, St. Helena Island. This island is off the coast of South Carolina, and its semi-isolation makes it an interesting field for the study of Negro songs. Ballanta's work is prefaced by a valuable but somewhat pedantic discussion of Negro music.

BURLIN, NATALIE CURTIS, *Negro Folk-Songs.* G. Schirmer, New York, 1918-19. Four small volumes of Negro songs recorded at Hampton Institute. Volumes I and II are spirituals, volumes III and IV are work songs and play songs. These songs are of special value in that the late Mrs. Burlin came nearer than any one else to the accurate reproduction of Negro songs in musical notation.

CAMPBELL, OLIVE DAME, and SHARP, CECIL J., *English Folk Songs from the Southern Appalachians.* The student who is interested in the origin of Negro songs and their relation to English folk songs will find valuable data in this book.

COX, J. H., *Folk Songs of the South.* Harvard University Press, 1924. Most of these songs are songs of the whites of the mountains, but they are particularly valuable in that they throw light on the origin of many Negro songs.

FENNER, T. P., *Religious Folk Songs of the American Negro.* Hampton Institute Press, 1924. (Arranged in 1909 by the Musical Directors of Hampton Normal and Industrial Institute

---

[1] This bibliography is not intended to cover all that has been written on Negro songs. It includes references to actual collections of songs and to a few other contributions which are of value to the serious student of Negro songs. Dozens of merely appreciative articles have been omitted. For a larger bibliography one may consult the latest issue of the *Negro Year Book.*

from the original edition by Thomas P. Fenner. Reprinted in 1924.) This volume contains the words and music of 153 religious songs.

FENNER, T. P., and RATHBUN, F. G., *Cabin and Plantation Songs*. New York, 1891. Old Negro plantation songs with music.

HALLOWELL, EMILY, *Calhoun Plantation Songs*. New York, 1910. A number of songs with music collected from the singing of Negroes on the Calhoun plantation.

HARRIS, JOEL CHANDLER, *Uncle Remus, His Songs and Sayings*. New York, 1880. Nine songs.

HARRIS, JOEL CHANDLER, *Uncle Remus and His Friends*. New York, 1892. Sixteen songs.

HIGGINSON, THOMAS WENTWORTH, *Army Life in a Black Regiment*. Boston, 1870. Chapter IX of this book is devoted to Negro spirituals as they were sung in Col. Higginson's regiment during the Civil War.

HOBSON, ANNE, *In Old Alabama*. New York, 1903. Ten dialect stories and songs.

JOHNSON, JAMES WELDON, *The Book of American Negro Spirituals*. Viking Press, New York, 1925. A collection of sixty-one spirituals. Most of these songs have been published in other collections, but the musical arrangements in this volume are new. While the melodies of the old songs are retained intact, an effort has been made to improve the rhythmic qualities of the accompaniments. The preface of the book is devoted to the origin, development, and appreciation of Negro spirituals.

KENNEDY, R. EMMET, *Black Cameos*. A. & C. Boni, New York, 1924. A collection of twenty-eight stories, mostly humorous, with songs interwoven. The words and music of seventeen songs are given.

KENNEDY, R. EMMET, *Mellows: Work Songs, Street Cries and Spirituals*. A. & C. Boni, New York, 1925. Several spirituals and street songs from New Orleans. The author includes character sketches of his singers. His discussion of the relation ofNegro songs to printed ballad sheets is especially interesting.

KREHBIEL, H. E., *Afro-American Folk Songs*. G. Schirmer, New York and London, 1914. A careful study of Negro folk songs from the point of view of the skilled musician. Songs and music from Africa and other sources are analyzed and compared with American Negro productions. The music of sixty or more songs and dance airs is given.

Marsh, J. B. T., *The Story of the Jubilee Singers.* Boston 1880. An account of the Jubilee Singers, with their songs.

Odum, Howard W., and Johnson, Guy B., *The Negro and His Songs.* University of North Carolina Press, Chapel Hill, 1925. A study of the origin and characteristic of Negro songs from the historical and sociological point of view. The words of 200 songs are given. The songs are discussed under three general classes: spirituals, social songs, and work songs.

Peterson, C. G., *Creole Songs from New Orleans.* New Orleans, 1902.

Pike, G. D., *The Jubilee Singers.* Boston and New York, 1873. Sixty-one religious songs.

Scarborough, Dorothy, *On the Trail of Negro Folk-Songs.* Harvard University Press, Cambridge, 1925. One of the most important contributions yet made to the study of Negro songs. This book presents some 200 secular songs, including the music of most of them. Especially interesting is the chapter on "The Negro's part in the Transmission of Traditional Songs and Ballads." The lack of any sort of index somewhat decreases the value of the book for purposes of reference and comparison.

Talley, Thomas W., *Negro Folk Rhymes.* Macmillan, New York, 1922. This volume contains about 350 rhymes and songs and a study of the origin, development, and characteristics of Negro rhymes. Besides a general index of songs, a comparative index is included.

Work, John Wesley, *Folk Songs of the American Negro.* Fisk University Press, Nashville, 1915. The words of fifty-five songs and music of nine, together with a study of the origin and growth of certain songs.

PERIODICALS

Adventure Magazine. The files of this magazine for the last few years should be of considerable interest to the student of folk song. A department called "Old Songs That Men Have Sung" is conducted by Dr. R. W. Gordon, a Harvard-trained student of folk song. Many of the songs printed in this department are Negro songs or Negro adaptions.

Backus, E. M., "Negro Songs from Georgia," *Journal of American Folk-Lore*, vol. 10, pp. 116, 202, 216; vol. 11, pp. 22, 60. Six religious songs.

Backus, E. M., "Christmas Carols from Georgia," *Journal of American Folk-Lore*, vol. 12, p. 272. Two songs.

Barton, W. E., "Hymns of Negroes," *New England Magazine*, vol. 19, pp. 669 et seq., 706 et seq. A number of songs with some musical notation and discussion.

Bergen, Mrs. F. D., "On the Eastern Shore," *Journal of American Folk-Lore*, vol. 2, pp. 296-298. Two fragments, with a brief discussion of the Negroes of the eastern shore of Maryland.

Brown, J. M., "Songs of the Slave," *Lippincotts*, vol. 2, pp. 617-623. Several songs with brief comments.

Cable, George W., "Creole Slave Songs," *Century*, vol. 31, pp. 807-828. Twelve songs with some fragments, music of seven.

Clarke, Mary Almsted, "Song Games of Negro Children in Virginia," *Journal of American Folk-Lore*, vol. 3, pp. 288-290. Nine song games and rhymes.

Cox, J. H., "John Hardy," *Journal of American Folk-Lore*, vol. 32, p. 505 et seq. Here will be found Cox's discussion of the John Hardy or John Henry story, together with several versions of the song.

Garnett, L. A., "Spirituals," *Outlook*, vol. 30, p. 589. Three religious songs. However, they appear to have been polished considerably by the writer.

Haskell, M. A., "Negro Spirituals," *Century*, vol. 36, pp. 577 et seq. About ten songs with music.

Higginson, T. W., "Hymns of Negroes," *Atlantic Monthly*, vol. 19, pp. 685 et seq. Thirty-six religious and two secular songs, with musical notation.

Lemmerman, K., "Improvised Negro Songs," *New Republic* vol. 13, pp. 214-215. Six religious songs or improvised fragments.

Lomax, J. A., "Self-pity in Negro Folk Song," *Nation*, vol. 105, pp. 141-145. About twenty songs, some new, others quoted from Perrow and Odum, with discussion.

"Negro Hymn of Day of Judgment," *Journal of American Folk-Lore*, vol. 9, p. 210. One religious song.

NILES, ABBE, "Blue Notes," *New Republic*, vol. 45, pp. 292-3. A discussion of the significance of the blues and the music of the blues. The style is somewhat too verbose and technical for the average reader.

ODUM, ANNA K., "Negro Folk Songs from Tennessee," *Journal of American Folk-Lore*, vol. 27, pp. 255-265. Twenty-one religious and four secular songs.

ODUM, HOWARD W., "Religious Folk Songs of the Southern Negroes," *Journal of Religious Psychology and Education*, vol. 3, pp. 265-365. About one hundred songs.

ODUM, HOWARD W., "Folk Song and Folk Poetry as Found in the Secular Songs of the Southern Negroes," *Journal of American Folk-Lore*, vol. 35, pp. 223-249; 351-396. About 120 songs.

ODUM, HOWARD W., "Swing Low, Sweet Chariot." *Country Gentleman*, March, 1926, pp. 18-19; 49-50. Several religious songs with discussion.

ODUM, HOWARD W., "Down that Lonesome Road." *Country Gentleman*, May, 1926, pp. 18-19, 79. Several secular songs, music of six, some new and some quoted from *The Negro and His Songs* and from the present collection.

PEABODY, CHARLES, "Notes on Negro Music," *Journal of American Folk-Lore*, vol. 16, pp. 148-52. Observations on the technique of the Negro workman in the South, with some songs and music.

PERKINS, A. E., "Spirituals from the Far South," *Journal of of American Folk-Lore*, vol. 35, pp. 223-249. Forty-seven songs.

PERROW, E. C., "Songs and Rhymes from the South," *Journal of American Folk-Lore*, vol. 25, pp. 137-155; vol. 26, pp. 123-173; vol. 28, pp. 129-190. A general collection containing 118 Negro songs, mostly secular.

REDFEARN, S. F., "Songs from Georgia," *Journal of American Folk-Lore*, vol. 34, pp. 121-124. One secular and three religious songs.

SPEERS, M. W. F., "Negro Songs and Folk-Lore," *Journal of American Folk-Lore*, vol. 23, pp. 435-439. One religious and one secular song.

STEWARD, T. G., "Negro Imagery," *New Republic*, vol. 12, p. 248. One religious improvisation, with discussion.

Thanet, Octave, "Cradle Songs of Negroes in North Carolina," *Journal of American Folk-Lore*, vol. 7, p. 310. Two lullabies.

Truitt, Florence, "Songs from Kentucky," *Journal of American Folk-Lore*, vol. 36, pp. 376-379. Four white songs, one of which contains several verses often found in Negro songs.

Webb, W. P., "Notes on Folk-Lore of Texas," *Journal of American Folk-Lore*, vol. 28, pp. 290-299. Five secular songs.

INDEX TO SONGS